A gift for

_____

from

_____

date

_____

An Inspirational Daily Planner 2009

THOMAS NELSON
Since 1798

NASHVILLE DALLAS MEXICO CITY RIO DE JANEIRO BEIJING

AN INSPIRATIONAL DAILY PLANNER 2009

© 2008

Published in Nashville, Tennessee, by Thomas Nelson. Thomas Nelson is a registered trademark of Thomas Nelson, Inc.

Thomas Nelson, Inc. titles may be purchased in bulk for educational, business, fundraising, or sales promotional use. For information, please e-mail SpecialMarkets@ThomasNelson.com.

Unless noted otherwise, all Scripture references in this book are from the *New King James Version* © 1979, 1980, 1982, 1992, 2002 Thomas Nelson, Inc., Publisher. Used by permission. Other Scripture references are from the following sources: Holy Bible, *New International Version*®. NIV® (NIV). © 1973, 1978, 1984 by the International Bible Society. Used by permission of Zondervan Publishing House. *The Message* (MSG), © by Eugene H. Peterson 1993, 1994, 1995. Used by permission of NavPress Publishing Group. The Holy Bible, *New Living Translation* (NLT), © 1996. Used by permission of Tyndale House Publishers, Inc., Wheaton, Illinois 60189. All rights reserved.

Project Manager: MacKenzie Clark Howard
Project Editor: Terri Gibbs
Designed by: Lori Lynch, Mary Hooper
Gretchen Stibolt at www.thedesigndesk.com

ISBN 10: 1-4041-8705-7 [5 X 7 orange/linen]
ISBN 13: 978-1-4041-8705-4
ISBN 10: 1-4041-8704-9 [5 X 7 floral]
ISBN 13: 978-1-4041-8704-7
ISBN 10: 1-4041-8703-0 [6.5 X 8.5 black]
ISBN 13: 978-1-4041-8703-0
ISBN 10: 1-4041-8702-2 [6.5 X 8.5 green/linen]
ISBN 13: 978-1-4041-8702-3

www.thomasnelson.com

Printed and bound in China

INTRODUCTION

The story is told that the fellow who invented Velcro got the idea when he was walking through a field one day. Rather than being simply irritated with all the little weed burrs that stuck to his pants, he studied them carefully and discovered something useful. Now that's wisdom: looking for the good in annoying, even uncomfortable situations.

The theme of this planner is everyday wisdom. Each minute of each hour of each day is a gift from God, a unique opportunity to live a meaningful and fulfilling life. Every day is also a challenge: we have places to go, people to see, things to do, and choices to make. But we do not face the daily dilemmas of life alone, for our Lord has promised to provide all the wisdom and insight we need, not just for major decisions but even for the smallest, simplest choices—like looking for something good in a weed burr.

This planner is designed to help organize your daily life—to serve as a reminder of schedules and meetings, or perhaps as a place to record your daily devotional thoughts and prayers.

May you live each day of this year to the fullest measure of God's love and wisdom.

CONTENTS

JANUARY 2009

MONDAY	TUESDAY	WEDNESDAY
5	6	7
TWELFTH NIGHT	EPIPHANY (IT., SP.)	
12	13	14
19	20	21
MARTIN LUTHER KING JR. DAY (U.S.)		
26	27	28
AUSTRALIA DAY (AUST.) CHINESE NEW YEAR		

THURSDAY	FRIDAY	SATURDAY/SUNDAY
1	2	3
		4
New Year's Day		
8	9	10
		11
15	16	17
		18
22	23	24
		25
		Sanctity of Human Life Sunday
29	30	31

If you want the good life, get wisdom. And if you want wisdom, get God.

—GEORGE O. WOOD

JANUARY

JANUARY

Thursday

1

Cast your burden on the LORD,
And He shall sustain you.
Psalm 55:22a

_____

_____

_____

_____

_____

With every catastrophe comes this gift—the opportunity
to see God at work in our lives.
—JAN WINEBRENNER

Friday

2

And my tongue shall sing aloud of Your righteousness.
Psalm 51:14b

_____

_____

_____

_____

_____

God is most glorified in you when you are most satisfied in Him.
—ARCHIBALD D. HART

JANUARY

Saturday

3

_____

_____

_____

_____

_____

_____

The greatest gift you can give your children is not
your riches, but revealing to them their own.
—MAX LUCADO

_____

Sunday

4

_____

_____

_____

_____

_____

_____

When God created the rabbit, it couldn't
have been with a straight face.
—AGNIESZKA TENNANT

_____

JANUARY

Monday

5

I love those who love me,
And those who seek me dilligently will find me.
Proverbs 8:17

_____

_____

_____

_____

_____

The most spiritual activity you will engage
in today is making choices.
—ERWIN MCMANUS

_____

Tuesday

6

Pursue peace with all people, and holiness,
without which no one will see the Lord.
Hebrews 12:14

_____

_____

_____

_____

_____

Pursuing pleasure in God is what we were created for.
—ARCHIBALD D. HART

_____

JANUARY

Listen to counsel and receive instruction,
That you may be wise in your latter days.
Proverbs 19:20

Choice without regret is a wonderful thing.
—JAN SILVIOUS

I press toward the goal for the prize of the
upward call of God in Christ Jesus.
Philippians 3:14

One does not become holy all at once.
—BROTHER LAWRENCE

JANUARY

Friday

9

Be filled with the Spirit, . . . singing and making melody in your heart to the Lord.
Ephesians 5:18b-19

_____

_____

_____

_____

_____

God has a mind to make you laugh.
—JOHN BUNYAN

Saturday

10

In everything give thanks; for this is the will of God in Christ Jesus for you.
1 Thessalonians 5:18

_____

_____

_____

_____

_____

God is going to do whatever He has to do in order to get you to heaven.
—ANTHONY DESTEFANO

JANUARY

*Now may the God of peace Himself
sanctify you completely.
1 Thessalonians 5:23a*

We are called to be down-to-earth as Christians
but not to be earthbound.
—OS GUINNESS

*A broken and a contrite heart—
These, O God, You will not despise.
Psalm 51:17b*

If our hopes are being disappointed just now,
it means they are being purified.
—OSWALD CHAMBERS

JANUARY

Tuesday
13

*Continue earnestly in prayer, being vigilant
in it with thanksgiving.*
Colossians 4:2

Is prayer your steering wheel or your spare tire?
—CORRIE TEN BOOM

Wednesday
14

*Now this is the confidence that we have in Him, that if
we ask anything according to His will, He hears us.*
1 John 5:14

God needs people He can count on to cross the finish line.
—DAVID EGNER

JANUARY

Ask, and it will be given to you; seek, and you will
find; knock, and it will be opened to you.
Matthew 7:7

God's answers are wiser than our prayers.
—ANONYMOUS

I waited patiently for the LORD;
And He inclined to me, And heard my cry.
Psalm 40:1

Patience is the companion of wisdom.
—ST. AUGUSTINE

JANUARY

Saturday

17

*Most assuredly, I say to you, he who believes in Me,
the works that I do he will do also.
John 14:12a*

_____

_____

_____

_____

_____

_____

_____

If God can work through me, He can work through anyone.
—ST. FRANCIS OF ASSISI

Sunday

18

*Then Peter said, "See, we have left all and followed you."
Luke 18:28*

_____

_____

_____

_____

_____

_____

The Bible is a book of *examples* of what it
looks like to walk with God.
—JOHN ELDREDGE

JANUARY

Be anxious for nothing, but in everything by prayer and . . .
with thanksgiving, let your requests be made known to God.
Philippians 4:6

One of our strongest callings as parents is to be prayer
warriors for our children rather than worry warriors.
—KAREN MAUDLIN

Do not set your mind on high things, but associate with
the humble. Do not be wise in your own opinion.
Romans 12:16

To be great in little things . . . is a virtue so rare
as to be worthy of canonization.
—HARRIET BEECHER STOWE

JANUARY

Wednesday

21

As for God, His way is perfect; The word of the LORD is proven; He is a shield to all who trust in Him.
Psalm 18:30

Aim at heaven and you will get earth thrown in.
Aim at earth and you will get neither.
—C. S. LEWIS

Thursday

22

"Comfort, yes, comfort My people!" Says your God.
Isaiah 40:1

We can be sure of God's consolation in our trials,
of His hope in our despair.
—MARVA DAWN

JANUARY

But as for you, you meant evil against me;
but God meant it for good.
Genesis 50:20a

With God all things are possible. Even
when the unimaginable occurs.
—JAN WINEBRENNER

We are the clay, and You our potter;
And all we are the work of Your hand.
Isaiah 64:8b

We are all different, because God made us that way.
—BILLY GRAHAM

JANUARY

Sunday

25

I have not departed from Your judgments,
for You Yourself have taught me.
Psalm 119:102

_____

_____

_____

_____

_____

_____

_____

Here's a radical idea: next time you're tempted to complain
about your work, praise God for it instead.
—MARK BUCHANAN

_____

Monday

26

Rejoice because your names are written in heaven.
Luke 10:20b

_____

_____

_____

_____

_____

_____

Grace teaches us that God loves because of who God is,
not because of who we are.
—PHILIP YANCEY

_____

*For if you forgive men their trespasses, your
heavenly Father will also forgive you.*
Matthew 6:14

When we genuinely forgive, we set a prisoner free and then
discover that the prisoner we set free was us.
—LEWIS SMEDES

*And forgive us our debts,
As we forgive our debtors.*
Matthew 6:12

Forgiveness is not about feeling. It's about willing.
—BETH MOORE

JANUARY

Thursday
29

He who is of a proud heart stirs up strife,
But he who trusts in the LORD will be prospered.
Proverbs 28:25

_____

_____

_____

_____

_____

Honoring God's ways and living for man's awe
are mutually incompatible goals.
—ALICIA BRITT CHOLE

Friday
30

Now faith is the substance of things hoped for,
the evidence of things not seen.
Hebrews 11:1

_____

_____

_____

_____

_____

Faith is the opposite of hype; it is heartbeat.
—LEONARD SWEET

JANUARY

A friend loves at all times.
Proverbs 17:17a

_____

_____

_____

_____

_____

_____

_____

_____

_____

_____

_____

_____

_____

_____

_____

_____

_____

_____

_____

The important thing is not to think much but to love much.
—ST. TERESA OF AVILA

_____

FEBRUARY 2009

MONDAY	TUESDAY	WEDNESDAY
2	3	4
CANDLEMAS		
9	10	11
16	17	18
FAMILY DAY (CAN.) PRESIDENT'S DAY		
23	24	25
	SHROVE TUESDAY	ASH WEDNESDAY

THURSDAY	FRIDAY	SATURDAY/SUNDAY
		1
5	6	7
		8
	WAITANGI DAY (NZ)	
12	13	14
		VALENTINE'S DAY (U.S., CAN.)
		15
LINCOLN'S BIRTHDAY (U.S.)		
19	20	21
		22
		TRANSFIGURATION SUNDAY
		WASHINGTON'S BIRTHDAY (U.S.)
26	27	28

God daily deposits
into our account of life
86,400 fleeting seconds,
1,400 precious minutes,
and 24 shining hours.

—HENRY GARIEPY

FEBRUARY

FEBRUARY

Sunday

1

Not My will, but Yours, be done.
Luke 22:42b

_____

_____

_____

_____

_____

_____

_____

In the complete surrender of His will to the will of the Father,
Christ's obedience reached its highest perfection.
—ANDREW MURRAY

Monday

2

But those who wait on the LORD shall renew their
strength; . . . they shall walk and not faint.
Isaiah 40:31

_____

_____

_____

_____

_____

_____

When God's power invades our lives we can do
things we never thought possible.
—NEIL CLARK WARREN

FEBRUARY

Let your conduct be without covetousness; be
content with such things as you have.
Hebrews 13:5a

3

Get all you can, save all you can, and give all you can.
—JOHN WESLEY

How precious also are Your thoughts to me,
O God! How great is the sum of them!
Psalm 139:17

4

If God does not give us what we crave,
He will give us what we need.
—THOMAS WATSON

FEBRUARY

Thursday

5

*There is no other name under heaven given among men
by which we must be saved.
Acts 4:12b*

Destiny is not a matter of chance, it is a matter of choice.
—WILLIAM J. BRYAN

Friday

6

*And let the beauty of the LORD our God be upon us,
And establish the work of our hands for us.
Psalm 90:17a*

He who is filled with love is filled with God.
—ST. AUGUSTINE

FEBRUARY

So teach us to number our days,
That we may gain a heart of wisdom.
Psalm 90:12

No gift is more precious than good advice.
—ERASMUS

Beloved, let us love one another, for love is of God;
and everyone who loves is born of God and knows God.
1 John 4:7

We must love ourselves if we're going to be
any good at loving others.
—LEITH ANDERSON

FEBRUARY

Monday

9

The LORD takes pleasure in those who fear Him,
In those who hope in His mercy.
Psalm 147:11

Meekness is a preference for God's will.
—A. T. PIERSON

Tuesday

10

Most assuredly, I say to you, he who hears My word and
believes in Him who sent Me has everlasting life.
John 5:24a

The Bible expresses the mind of God since God Himself
speaks to us through its pages.
—DALLAS WILLARD

FEBRUARY

Your mercy, O LORD, is in the heavens; Your faithfulness
reaches to the clouds.
Psalm 36:5

God is willing to make the impossibly difficult decisions
that are beyond our experience and wisdom.
—LEITH ANDERSON

And this is the promise that He
has promised us—eternal life.
1 John 2:25

Fear vanishes when it is exposed to the promises of God's Word.
—BILLY GRAHAM

FEBRUARY

Friday

13

*The eternal God is your refuge, and underneath
are the everlasting arms.
Deuteronomy 33:27a*

No life ever grows great until it is focused,
dedicated, and disciplined.
—ANONYMOUS

Saturday

14

*Do not fear, little flock, for it is your Father's good
pleasure to give you the kingdom.
Luke 12:32*

Courage arises from those who place the
needs of others before themselves.
—JEFF O'LEARY

FEBRUARY

And He said to them, "You are from beneath; I am from above. You are of this world; I am not of this world."
John 8:23

No one, nor anything, is mightier than Jesus!
—ANNE GRAHAM LOTZ

This is the day the LORD has made;
We will rejoice and be glad in it.
Psalm 118:24

There has never been another day just like today, and there will never be another just like it again.
—FREDERICK BUECHNER

FEBRUARY

Tuesday

17

Greater love has no one than this, than to lay down one's life for his friends.
John 15:13

_____

_____

_____

_____

_____

_____

I suspect that if we were convinced of God's personal love for us, few of us could resist it.
—BETH BOORAM

Wednesday

18

Lo, I am with you always, even to the end of the age. Amen.
Matthew 28:20

_____

_____

_____

_____

_____

God is not alien to the circumstances of our lives but comes to us in them.
—DAVID BENNER

FEBRUARY

*I called on the Lord in distress; the Lord answered
me and set me in a broad place.*
Psalm 118:5

The deep fear lying behind every loss is that we have been
abandoned by the God who should have saved us.
—CRAIG BARNES

---

*The Lord is near to all who call upon Him,
To all who call upon Him in truth.*
Psalm 145:18

Friday
20

God welcomes our prayers. He is much more concerned
about our hearts than our eloquence.
—BILLY GRAHAM

FEBRUARY

Saturday
21

Come to Me, all you who labor and are heavy laden, and I will give you rest.
Matthew 11:28

_____

_____

_____

_____

_____

The person who is prepared to put his life in the
Master's hands has found the place of rest.
—PHILLIP KELLER

Sunday
22

But you, O man of God, flee these things and pursue righteousness, godliness, faith, love, patience, gentleness.
1 Timothy 6:11

_____

_____

_____

_____

_____

One of the best legacies a father can leave his
children is to love their mother.
—C. NEIL STRAIT

FEBRUARY

The counsel of the LORD stands forever,
The plans of His heart to all generations.
Psalm 33:11

The will of God comes from the heart of God.
—WARREN WIERSBE

And the Lord will deliver me from every evil work and
preserve me for His heavenly kingdom.
2 Timothy 4:18a

Spiritual maturity is the quiet confidence that God is in control.
—CHARLES R. SWINDOLL

FEBRUARY

25

But You are holy,
Enthroned in the praises of Israel.
Psalm 22:3

_____

_____

_____

_____

_____

We may not always understand God's ways, but
because He is holy we can trust Him.
—HENRY GARIEPY

Thursday

26

For we have great joy and consolation in your love, because
the hearts of the saints have been refreshed by you, brother.
Philemon 1:7

_____

_____

_____

_____

_____

Anyone who lives a life full of love will be joyful.
—MIKE MASON

FEBRUARY

He fashions their hearts individually;
He considers all their works.
Psalm 33:15

Friday

27

You are heaven's custom design.
—MAX LUCADO

As the mountains surround Jerusalem, so the
LORD surrounds His people.
Psalm 125:2a

Saturday

28

Behind whatever happens is a God who cares.
—CHARLES R. SWINDOLL

MARCH 2009

MONDAY	TUESDAY	WEDNESDAY
2	3	4
9	10 Purim	11
16	17 St. Patrick's Day	18
23	24	25
30	31	

THURSDAY	FRIDAY	SATURDAY/SUNDAY
		1
5	6	7
		8
12	13	14
		15
19	20	21
		Juarez Birthday (Mex.)
		22
	Spring Begins	Mothering Sunday (UK)
26	27	28
		29

The happiest people I know are the ones who have given the worrisome details of their lives into God's keeping.

—CHARLES R. SWINDOLL

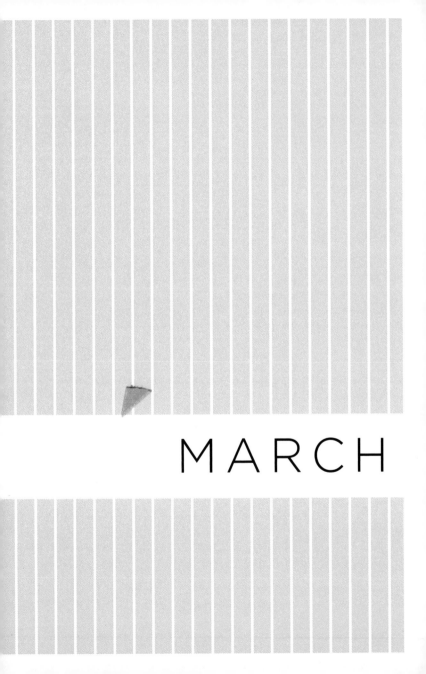

MARCH

MARCH

Sunday

1

You will keep him in perfect peace, Whose mind is stayed on You, Because he trusts in You.
Isaiah 26:3

Faith is permitting ourselves to be seized
by the things we do not see.
—MARTIN LUTHER

Monday

2

For it is God who works in you both to will and to do for His good pleasure.
Philippians 2:13

It is the work that God does through us that counts,
not what we do for Him.
—OSWALD CHAMBERS

50

MARCH

And now, Lᴏʀᴅ, what do I wait for?
My hope is in You.
Psalm 39:7

3

The difference between believers and atheists is not that believers
suffer any less—they don't—it's that they suffer *with hope*.
—ANTHONY DESTEFANO

My heart is steadfast, O God, my heart is
steadfast; I will sing and give praise.
Psalm 57:7

4

If faith is a radical reliance on God, it is undaunted
by circumstances, unaltered by the odds.
—OS GUINNESS

MARCH

Thursday

5

I have taught you in the way of wisdom;
I have led you in right paths.
Proverbs 4:11

God's ways are best, His words are true, His love is great,
and His faithfulness is absolute.
—JAN WINEBRENNER

Friday

6

He who heeds the word wisely will find good,
And whoever trusts in the LORD, happy is he.
Proverbs 16:20

We've been given one piece of life's jigsaw puzzle.
Only God has the cover of the box.
—MAX LUCADO

MARCH

For the world is Mine, and all its fullness.
Psalm 50:12b

The world is a book, and those who do not travel read only a page.
—ST. AUGUSTINE

And He Himself gave some to be apostles, some prophets,
some evangelists, and some pastors and teachers.
Ephesians 4:11

Our sense of self-worth is strengthened when we know that we
are each uniquely fashioned by God's infinite care.
—MARVA DAWN

MARCH

Monday
9

With the merciful You will show Yourself merciful.
2 Samuel 22:26a

Pride inverts the universe's deepest truth:
that we need and serve God.
—MARK BUCHANAN

Tuesday
10

You have commanded us
To keep Your precepts diligently.
Psalm 119:4

God's Word isn't to be debated or dissected; it is to be done.
—BILLY GRAHAM

MARCH

My little children, let us not love in word or
in tongue, but in deed and in truth.
1 John 3:18

11

Not to forgive imprisons me in the past and locks
out all potential for change.
—PHILLIP YANCEY

Trust in the Lord, and do good;
Dwell in the land, and feed on His faithfulness.
Psalm 37:3

12

God is not just a firm place to stand. He's a firm place to stay.
—BETH MOORE

55

MARCH

Friday

13

For I know the thoughts that I think toward you, says the L<small>ORD</small>, thoughts of peace and not evil, to give you a future and a hope. Jeremiah 29:11

God alone realizes our full potential and comprehends the longings in our souls.
—ALICIA BRITT CHOLE

Saturday

14

Love suffers long and is kind.
1 Corinthians 13:4a

The true character of love is self-giving.
—LEONARD SWEET

MARCH

You know my sitting down and my rising up;
You understand my thought afar off.
Psalm 139:2

When you trust God, everything about your life
becomes more joyful and more manageable.
—NEIL CLARK WARREN

He who has the Son has life.
1 John 5:12a

Never be afraid to trust an unknown future to a known God.
—CORRIE TEN BOOM

MARCH

Tuesday

17

And I will delight myself in Your commandments,
Which I love.
Psalm 119:47

The Holy Scriptures are our letters from home.
—ST. AUGUSTINE

Wednesday

18

Set your mind on things above,
not on things on the earth.
Colossians 3:2

Heaven will be the perfection we have always longed for.
—BILLY GRAHAM

MARCH

*And whatever you do, do it heartily, as to
the Lord and not to men.*
Colossians 3:23

Jesus is really the only boss a Christian worker has to please.
—LEITH ANDERSON

*The righteousness of the blameless
will direct his way aright.*
Proverbs 11:5a

Integrity is formed, not born, one decision at a time.
—JEFF O'LEARY

MARCH

Saturday

21

I sought the LORD, and he answered me;
he delivered me from all my fears.
Psalm 34:4 NIV

_____

_____

_____

_____

_____

_____

The antidote to fear is faith.
—ANNE GRAHAM LOTZ

Sunday

22

He who promised is faithful.
Hebrews 10:23b

_____

_____

_____

_____

_____

_____

By far, the most important thing about praying is to keep at it.
—FREDERICK BUECHNER

MARCH

He does great things past finding out,
Yes, wonders without number.
Job 9:10

Monday

23

We like pat answers because they seem
more certain than a mysterious God.
—BETH BOORAM

A man who has friends must himself be friendly.
Proverbs 18:24a

Tuesday

24

Who is the person rich in friends and affection?
The one willing to give himself away to others.
—PHILLIP KELLER

MARCH

Wednesday

25

Worship the LORD in the beauty of holiness.
Psalm 29:2b

Holiness is Christlikeness—being conformed to
His love, His purity, His character.
—HENRY GARIEPY

Thursday

26

But let each one examine his own work, and then he will
have rejoicing in himself alone, and not in another.
Galatians 6:4

God never called you to be anyone other than you.
—MAX LUCADO

MARCH

Then our mouth was filled with laughter,
and our tongue with singing.
Psalm 126:2a

27

Laughter—I don't know of a more contagious sound.
—CHARLES R. SWINDOLL

Let us therefore come boldly to the throne of grace, that we
may obtain mercy and find grace to help in time of need.
Hebrews 4:16

28

God has the grace to give me what I need,
and the grace to not. He's full of grace.
—MARY GRAHAM

MARCH

Sunday

29

Be still, and know that I am God.
Psalm 46:10a

For most of us, Sabbath will not become possible without
extensive, regular practice of solitude.
—DALLAS WILLARD

Monday

30

Blessed be the God and Father of our Lord Jesus Christ,
the Father of mercies and God of all comfort.
2 Corinthians 1:3

God wants us to come to Him as we are: broken and
bruised with tear-stained faces.
—SHEILA WALSH

MARCH

Present your bodies a living sacrifice, holy, acceptable
to God, which is your reasonable service.
Romans 12:1b

31

God's will is the best way for me, though rarely the easiest.
—PHILIP YANCEY

APRIL 2009

MONDAY	TUESDAY	WEDNESDAY
		1
6	7	8
13	14	15
Easter Monday (Can., UK)	21	22
20	21	22 Administrative Professionals Day (U.S., Can.)
27	28	29

THURSDAY	FRIDAY	SATURDAY/SUNDAY
2	3	4
		5
		PALM SUNDAY
9	10	11
		12
MAUNDY THURSDAY		
PASSOVER	GOOD FRIDAY	EASTER
16	17	18
		19
23	24	25
		LIBERATION DAY (IT.)
		ANZAC DAY (AUST., NZ)
		26
30		
QUEEN'S BIRTHDAY (NETH.)		

God knows the whole story of your life. He knows the last chapter, and He thinks you're wonderful.

—JAN SILVIOUS

APRIL

APRIL

Wednesday

1

If anyone loves Me, he will keep My word; . . . and We will come to him and make our home with him.
John 14:23

Little choices make big goals become a reality.
—HENRY CLOUD & JOHN TOWNSEND

Thursday

2

The blameless in their ways are His delight.
Proverbs 11:20b

Integrity always matters. If for no other reason, because it matters to God.
—BRUCE BICKEL & STAN JANTZ

Friday

Sanctify them by Your truth. Your word is truth.
John 17:17

3

_____

_____

_____

_____

_____

_____

The Bible always points us in the right direction.
—RICHARD DE HAAN

_____

This is My commandment, that you love
one another as I have loved you.
John 15:12

Saturday

4

_____

_____

_____

_____

_____

_____

The true measure of God's love is that He loves without measure.
—DAVID EGNER

_____

APRIL

Sunday

5

If anyone serves Me, him My Father will honor.
John 12:26b

God never gives anyone too much to do. We do that to ourselves.
—DALLAS WILLARD

Monday

6

Be of good courage, And He shall strengthen your
heart, All you who hope in the LORD.
Psalm 31:24

Believing God truly cares is worth a fortune in
hope, victory, and spiritual rest.
—LUCI SWINDOLL

APRIL

7

Yet they seek Me daily, And delight to know My ways.
Isaiah 58:2a

_____

_____

_____

_____

_____

_____

In prayer we lean our heads upon God's breast.
We are both deeply heard and deeply understood.
—PATSY CLAIRMONT

Wednesday

8

I know that You can do everything,
And that no purpose of Yours can be withheld from You.
Job 42:2

_____

_____

_____

_____

_____

_____

Trust comes to those who take God at His Word.
—BETH MOORE

APRIL

Thursday
9

He who believes in Me, . . . out of his heart will flow rivers of living water.
John 7:38

God's plan is not designed to make us comfortable;
it's designed to make us more like Christ.
—CHARLES R. SWINDOLL

Friday
10

You will guide me with Your counsel,
And afterward receive me to glory.
Psalm 73:24

We kneel, only to find we rise taller.
—PHILIP YANCEY

Saturday

LORD, You have heard the desire of the humble.
Psalm 10:17a

11

If I am full of myself there is no way I can be full of God.
—RICHARD OWEN ROBERTS

Sunday

My help comes from the LORD,
Who made heaven and earth.
Psalm 121:2

12

When we pray we are on the glittering floor
of the great King's reception room.
—CHARLES SPURGEON

APRIL

Monday
13

Then God blessed the seventh day and sanctified it,
because in it He rested from all His work.
Genesis 2:3a

_____

_____

_____

_____

_____

_____

You can face life a day at a time if you use Sunday
wisely—breathing in God in big, big doses.
—JUNE MASTERS BACHER

Tuesday
14

Therefore my heart is glad, and my glory rejoices;
My flesh also will rest in hope.
Psalm 16:9

_____

_____

_____

_____

_____

_____

True security is not in the bank, but in the
assurance that God will take care of us.
—PHILLIP KELLER

*Having then gifts differing according to the grace
that is given to us, let us use them.*
Romans 12:6a

Choose satisfaction over salary. Better to be happy
with little than miserable with much.
—MAX LUCADO

*Whatever things are of good report . . .
meditate on these things.*
Philippians 4:8b

Negative self-talk is a powerful enemy of joy.
—MIKE MASON

APRIL

Friday

17

His descendants will be mighty on earth;
The generation of the upright will be blessed.
Psalm 112:2

The greatest legacy we can leave to the next
generation is our faith and trust in God.
—HENRY GARIEPY

Saturday

18

Let every man be swift to hear,
slow to speak, slow to wrath.
James 1:19b

Our mates are tailor-made by God to
complement us, not irritate us.
—ROBERT JEFFRESS

Ponder the path of your feet,
And let all your ways be established.
Proverbs 4:26

Sunday

19

Our days are too precious to be squandered
on our own selfish little selves.
—PHILLIP KELLER

You are He who took me out of my mother's womb.
My praise shall be continually of You.
Psalm 71:6

Monday

20

God had a choice about it, and He chose to give you life.
—BILLY GRAHAM

APRIL

Tuesday
21

Therefore You are great, O Lord GOD. For there is none like You.
2 Samuel 7:22a

_____

_____

_____

_____

_____

_____

God is faithful and consistent in nature but He is not predictable and calculated.
—BETH BOORAM

Wednesay
22

But he who sows righteousness will have a sure reward.
Proverbs 11:18b

_____

_____

_____

_____

_____

_____

Whatever real success you have will be measured in how well you please Christ, not anyone else.
—FREDERICK BUECHNER

Therefore comfort each other and edify one another,
just as you also are doing.
1 Thessalonians 5:11

_____

_____

_____

_____

_____

_____

_____

We need each other's encouragement and wisdom.
—BILLY GRAHAM

_____

And be kind to one another, tenderhearted, forgiving
one another, even as God in Christ forgave you.
Ephesians 4:32

_____

_____

_____

_____

_____

We forgive others, not because they deserve it,
but because Christ deserves it!
—ANNE GRAHAM LOTZ

_____

APRIL

Saturday

25

To seek one's own glory is not glory.
Proverbs 25:27b

_____

_____

_____

_____

_____

_____

There is no room for God in the heart that worships itself.
—JEFF O'LEARY

Sunday

26

You have commanded us
To keep Your precepts diligently.
Psalm 119:4

_____

_____

_____

_____

_____

We will be spiritually safe in our use of the Bible if we follow
a simple rule: Read with a submissive attitude.
—DALLAS WILLARD

APRIL

Forever, O LORD, Your word is settled in heaven.
Your faithfulness endures to all generations.
Psalm 119:89-90a

_____

_____

_____

_____

_____

_____

_____

Prayer is like a key that opens heaven to us on earth.
—LEITH ANDERSON

_____

Tuesday
28

Your hands have made me and fashioned me.
Psalm 119:73a

_____

_____

_____

_____

_____

_____

_____

Parents should help their children dream a big dream for their lives.
—NEIL CLARK WARREN

_____

APRIL

Wednesday

29

[Love] bears all things, believes all things, hopes all things, endures all things.
1 Corinthians 13:7

_____

_____

_____

_____

_____

_____

The dimensions of love are immeasurable.
—LEONARD SWEET

Thursday

30

And a man of understanding is of a calm spirit.
Proverbs 17:27b

_____

_____

_____

_____

_____

_____

Self-control is not conferred or awarded;
it is cultivated and accumulated.
—ALICIA BRITT CHOLE

PERSONAL NOTES

MAY 2009

MONDAY	TUESDAY	WEDNESDAY
4	5	6
	Cinco de Mayo	
May Day Holiday (UK)	Liberation Day (Neth.)	
11	12	13
18	19	20
Victoria Day (Can.)		
25	26	27
Memorial Day (U.S.)		
Spring Holiday (UK)		

THURSDAY	FRIDAY	SATURDAY/SUNDAY
	1	2
		3
7	8	9
		10
NATIONAL DAY OF PRAYER		MOTHER'S DAY (U.S.)
14	15	16
		ARMED FORCES DAY (U.S.)
		17
21	22	23
		24
ASCENSION DAY		
28	29	30
		31
		PENTECOST SUNDAY

With God,
every day matters,
every person counts.

—MAX LUCADO

MAY

MAY

Friday
1

Teach me Your way, O LORD;
I will walk in Your truth.
Psalm 86:11a

God is always speaking. But we're not always listening.
—MARK BUCHANAN

Saturday
2

This is love, that we walk according to His
commandments.
2 John 1:6a

You will never use your own volition more dramatically
than when you agree with God to start forgiving.
—BETH MOORE

*For the law was given through Moses, but grace
and truth came through Jesus Christ.*
John 1:17

Sunday

Grace means there is nothing we can do to
make God love us more—or love us less.
—PHILIP YANCEY

*Every man should eat and drink and enjoy the good
of all his labor—it is the gift of God.*
Ecclesiastes 3:13b

Monday

Everything we use and have and do is a gift on loan from God.
—MARVA DAWN

MAY

Tuesday

5

Oh, taste and see that the LORD is good;
Blessed is the man who trusts in Him!
Psalm 34:8

Always, God ultimately exceeds our hopes and dreams.
—JAN WINEBRENNER

Wednesday

6

I have come that they may have life, and that
they may have it more abundantly.
John 10:10 b

Whatever might be going on in your life, God always
has His eye on your transformation.
—JOHN ELDREDGE

Trust in Him at all times, you people; Pour out your heart before Him; God is a refuge for us. Selah.
Psalm 62:8

Faith that is sure of itself is not faith. Faith that is sure of God is the only faith there is.
—OSWALD CHAMBERS

Watch, stand fast in the faith, be brave, be strong.
1 Corinthians 16:13

People do not so much lose their faith as cease to use their faith.
—OS GUINNESS

MAY

Saturday

9

My people will dwell in a peaceful habitation,
In secure dwellings, and in quiet resting places.
Isaiah 32:18

_____

_____

_____

_____

_____

Next to faith this is the highest art—to be content with
the calling in which God has placed you.
—MARTIN LUTHER

Sunday

10

Breaking bread from house to house, they ate their
food with gladness and simplicity of heart.
Acts 2:46b

_____

_____

_____

_____

_____

There is something in humility that strangely exalts the heart.
—ST. AUGUSTINE

MAY

Let those who love Your salvation say
continually, "Let God be magnified!"
Psalm 70:4b

Prayer is not simply getting things from God; prayer
is getting into perfect communion with God.
—OSWALD CHAMBERS

He awakens Me morning by morning,
He awakens My ear To hear as the learned.
Isaiah 50:4b

God has placed obvious limits on our intelligence—but
none whatsoever on our stupidity.
—ANTHONY DESTEFANO

MAY

Wednesday

13

For no other foundation can anyone lay than that which is laid, which is Jesus Christ.
1 Corinthians 3:11

_____

_____

_____

_____

_____

_____

What you know and believe about God is the foundation
of every decision you'll make.
—JAN SILVIOUS

Thursday

14

He who gets wisdom loves his own soul.
Proverbs 19:8a

_____

_____

_____

_____

_____

_____

When you live wisely, you understand better how to live well.
—GEORGE O. WOOD

MAY

The righteous shall flourish like a palm tree.
Psalm 92:12a

_____

_____

_____

_____

_____

_____

It isn't your position that makes you happy
or unhappy. It's your disposition.
—BRUCE BICKEL & STAN JANTZ

The tongue of the wise promotes health.
Proverbs 12:18b

_____

_____

_____

_____

_____

There is nothing like the encouragement of a true friend.
—ANITA RENFROE

_____

MAY

Sunday
17

The mouth of the righteous is a well of life.
Proverbs 10:11a

Whiners neither enjoy nor give joy.
—PATSY CLAIRMONT

Monday
18

The wicked borrows and does not repay,
But the righteous shows mercy and gives.
Psalm 37:21

Mercy is an act of kindness. It is also an expression of tenderness.
—R. C. SPROUL

MAY

By this we know that we abide in Him, and He in us,
because He has given us of His Spirit.
1 John 4:13

19

We glorify God by reflecting the character of
God in the way we think and act.
—JAMES SIRE

Blessed are the merciful,
For they shall obtain mercy.
Matthew 5:7

Wednesday

20

When we extend mercy to the broken, we reach
out with the hands of Christ Himself.
—PHILIP YANCEY

MAY

Thursday

21

*In the house of the righteous
there is much treasure.
Proverbs 15:6a*

To be rich in God is better than to be rich in goods.
—DENNIS DE HAAN

Friday

22

*Now to Him who is able to do exceedingly abundantly
above all that we ask or think.
Ephesians 3:20a*

God always gives us what we ask for—or something better.
—HERBERT VANDER LUGT

MAY

*And let us consider one another in order
to stir up love and good works.*
Hebrews 10:24

In a good marriage, each partner understands and
protects the fragility of the other's heart.
—HENRY CLOUD & JOHN TOWNSEND

*The entirety of Your word is truth,
And every one of Your righteous judgments endures forever.*
Psalm 119:160

Jesus is eternally the same yesterday, today, and forever.
—ANNE GRAHAM LOTZ

MAY

Monday
25

Your Father knows the things you have need of before you ask Him.
Matthew 6:8b

_____

_____

_____

_____

_____

The fewer the words, the better the prayer.
—MARTIN LUTHER

Tuesday
26

If then God so clothes the grass, . . .
how much more will He clothe you?
Luke 12:28a

_____

_____

_____

_____

_____

Christ's remedy for worry is to be like the ravens
and lilies—trust God to do His job.
—BETH MOORE

But if we walk in the light as He is in the light,
we have fellowship with one another.
1 John 1:7a

_____

_____

_____

_____

_____

_____

_____

To forgive is to cultivate a garden filled with the
flowers of kindness and tenderness.
—KAREN KINGSBURY

Hide me under the shadow of Your wings.
Psalm 17:8b

_____

_____

_____

_____

_____

_____

Even in the midst of disappointment and surprise you will
discover how very secure you are in God's hands.
—CHARLES R. SWINDOLL

MAY

Friday

29

Believe in the LORD your God, and you shall be established; believe His prophets, and you shall prosper.
2 Chronicles 20:20b

This is the essence of trust: to be
convinced of the reliability of God.
—BRENNAN MANNING

Saturday

30

He who has begun a good work in you will complete it until the day of Jesus Christ.
Philippians 1:6b

In God it's never too late to be what you might have been.
—SHEILA WALSH

Come and see the works of God; He is awesome
in His doing toward the sons of men.
Psalm 66:5

God appreciates us for who we really are. So we can, too.
—LUCI SWINDOLL

JUNE 2009

MONDAY	TUESDAY	WEDNESDAY
1	2	3
QUEEN'S BIRTHDAY (NZ)	REPUBLIC DAY (IT.)	
8	9	10
15	16	17
22	23	24
		ST. JEAN BAPTISTE (QUEBEC)
29	30	
STS. PETER & PAUL DAY (IT., SP.)		

THURSDAY	FRIDAY	SATURDAY/SUNDAY
4	5	6
		7
		TRINITY SUNDAY
11	12	13
		14
CORPUS CHRISTI		FLAG DAY (U.S.)
18	19	20
		21
		SUMMER BEGINS
		FATHER'S DAY (U.S.)
25	26	27
		28

When we are caught up in the celebration of God, there is no room for negative living.

—LUCI SWINDOLL

JUNE

JUNE

Monday

1

Make a careful exploration of who you are and the work you have been given.
Galatians 6:4a MSG

You can do something no one else can do in a fashion no one else can do it.
—Max Lucado

Tuesday

2

I can do all things through Christ who strengthens me.
Philippians 4:13

At every point where we doubt ourselves, we really doubt God.
—Mike Mason

JUNE

*Let us come before His presence
with thanksgiving.
Psalm 95:2a*

Thankfulness is thoughtfulness.
—HENRY GARIEPY

*This is my beloved, and this is my friend,
O daughters of Jerusalem!
Song of Solomon 5:16b*

Successful marriage is always a triangle: a man, a woman, and God.
—CECIL MYERS

JUNE

Friday

5

God resists the proud,
But gives grace to the humble.
James 4:6b

_____

_____

_____

_____

_____

_____

Pride is a deification of self.
—J. OSWALD SANDERS

Saturday

6

And do not be conformed to this world, but be
transformed by the renewing of your mind.
Romans 12:2a

_____

_____

_____

_____

_____

The world urges us to "get, get, get." Christ comes
along and says, "Give, give, give."
—PHILLIP KELLER

JUNE

*The effective, fervent prayer of a
righteous man avails much.*
James 5:16b

The best way for a child to learn to pray is to live
with a father and mother who pray.
—JOHANN PESTALOZZI

*"I am the good shepherd. The good shepherd
gives His life for the sheep."*
John 10:11

God shepherds each one of us as an individual.
—BETH BOORAM

JUNE

9

He will be with you, He will not leave you nor forsake you; do not fear nor be dismayed.
Deuteronomy 31:8b

Christ is there with us on our way as
surely as the way itself is there.
—FREDERICK BUECHNER

Wednesday

10

By this we know love, because He laid down His life for us.
1 John 3:16a

When Christ's love fills our hearts it puts selfishness on the run.
—BILLY GRAHAM

Christ Jesus . . . is at the right hand
of God and is also interceding for us.
Romans 8:34b NIV

The God of the universe bends down to hear
what we have to say! And He answers!
—ANNE GRAHAM LOTZ

Rest in the LORD, and wait patiently for Him.
Psalm 37:7a

Time belongs to God. He has it all in the palm
of His hand, and He is never in a hurry.
—JEFF O'LEARY

JUNE

Saturday

13

Listen to my cry for help, my king and my God,
for to you I pray.
Psalm 5:2 NIV

_____

_____

_____

_____

_____

_____

_____

Prayer is the language of the soul.
—LEITH ANDERSON

Sunday

14

In the world you will have tribulation; but be
of good cheer, I have overcome the world.
John 16:33b

_____

_____

_____

_____

_____

_____

God never wastes suffering.
—WARREN WIERSBE

JUNE

Great is the LORD, and greatly to be praised;
And His greatness is unsearchable.
Psalm 145:3

More than anything else, God has impeccable integrity.
He is morally and ethically perfect.
—LEITH ANDERSON

I live by faith in the Son of God, who loved me
and gave Himself for me.
Galatians 2:20b

Faith is deliberate confidence in the character of God.
—OSWALD CHAMBERS

JUNE

Wednesday

17

The LORD is my shepherd; I shall not want.
Psalm 23:1

It is not my ability, but my response to God's ability that counts.
—CORRIE TEN BOOM

Thursday

18

And you, fathers, do not provoke your children to wrath, but
bring them up in the training and admonition of the Lord.
Ephesians 6:4

Show me great kids, and I will show you parents who
have loved and disciplined them with great care.
—NEIL CLARK WARREN

JUNE

A man's heart plans his way,
But the LORD directs his steps.
Proverbs 16:9

19

_____

_____

_____

_____

_____

_____

Jesus makes us wholly who we are—each one of us.
—LEONARD SWEET

_____

Saturday

All unrighteousness is sin.
1 John 5:17a

20

_____

_____

_____

_____

_____

_____

When we say yes to temptations, we are choosing
to feed sin that Jesus died for.
—ALICIA BRITT CHOLE

_____

JUNE

21

*There remains, then, a Sabbath-rest
for the people of God.
Hebrews 4:9 NIV*

Sabbath is the one day when the only thing you must
do is to not do the things you must.
—MARK BUCHANAN

22

*The LORD bless you and keep you.
Numbers 6:24*

Regardless who has betrayed you, God is
firm in His commitment to you.
—BETH MOORE

JUNE

No one is holy like the LORD.
1 Samuel 2:2a

All of God's dealings with us reflect
His holiness and perfect integrity.
—JAN WINEBRENNER

A generous man devises generous things,
And by generosity he shall stand.
Isaiah 32:8

An open heart produces open purse strings and
open refrigerators and open clocks.
—MARVA DAWN

JUNE

Thursday

25

I am the good shepherd; and I know My sheep, and am known by My own.
John 10:14

_____

_____

_____

_____

_____

_____

The Bible is the story of God seeking us out, calling us back to Himself.
—JOHN ELDREDGE

Friday

26

You yourselves are taught by God to love one another.
1 Thessalonians 4:9b

_____

_____

_____

_____

_____

Love is the beauty of the soul.
—ST. AUGUSTINE

JUNE

Let my prayer be set before You as incense.
Psalm 141:2a

The meaning of prayer is that we get
hold of God, not of the answer.
—OSWALD CHAMBERS

If any of you lacks wisdom, let him ask of God, . . .
and it will be given to him.
James 1:5

Sunday

28

Solomon's wisdom was the gift of God to a
man humble enough to ask for it.
—GEORGE O. WOOD

JUNE

Monday

29

You are my hiding place and my shield;
I hope in Your word.
Psalm 119:114

God's word to us is joy in the midst of sorrow and pain,
peace in the midst of tension and anxiety.
—MARVA DAWN

Tuesday

30

The world of the generous gets larger and larger.
Proverbs 11:24a MSG

Those who store up treasure only on earth discover, too late,
that such storage is merely composting.
—MARK BUCHANAN

PERSONAL NOTES

_____

_____

_____

_____

_____

_____

_____

_____

_____

_____

_____

_____

_____

_____

_____

_____

_____

_____

_____

_____

_____

_____

JULY 2009

MONDAY	TUESDAY	WEDNESDAY
		1 Canada Day (Can.)
6	7	8
13	14 Bastille Day (Fr.)	15
20	21 National Day (Belg.)	22
27	28	29

THURSDAY	FRIDAY	SATURDAY/SUNDAY
2	3	4
		INDEPENDENCE DAY (U.S.)
		5
9	10	11
		12
16	17	18
		19
23	24	25
		ST. JAMES DAY (SP.)
		26
30	31	

God not only put us on this journey but He wants to join us on it, if we will only let Him.

—BILLY GRAHAM

JULY

JULY

Wednesday

1

The LORD is gracious and full of compassion,
Slow to anger and great in mercy.
Psalm 145:8

_____

_____

_____

_____

_____

_____

God's love reaches as far down as humans can go.
—LEONARD SWEET

Thursday

2

And my soul shall be joyful in the LORD;
It shall rejoice in His salvation.
Psalm 35:9

_____

_____

_____

_____

_____

A joyful heart is the normal result of a heart burning with love.
—MOTHER TERESA

JULY

*Let Your lovingkindness and Your
truth continually preserve me.
Psalm 40:11b*

Choosing truth not only makes a difference,
it makes a difference that blesses our future.
—ALICIA BRITT CHOLE

*I must work the works of Him who
sent Me while it is day.
John 9:4a*

God is always at the center of the wise spiritual quest.
—NEIL CLARK WARREN

JULY

Sunday

5

Therefore, as we have opportunity, let us do good to all.
Galatians 6:10a

When God speaks of love, He speaks of
love as being a choice we make.
—LEITH ANDERSON

Monday

6

A man can do nothing better than to eat and drink
and find satisfaction in his work.
Ecclesiastes 2:24a NIV

Instead of seeing your job as a burden, see it as a
responsibility given you by God.
—BILLY GRAHAM

JULY

The fear of the LORD is the instruction of wisdom,
And before honor is humility.
Proverbs 15:33

7

_____

_____

_____

_____

_____

_____

_____

Daily, we are becoming reflections of what we say and do.
—JEFF O'LEARY

_____

And if I go and prepare a place for you, I will come back
and take you to be with me that you also may be where I am.
John 14:3 NIV

Wednesday

8

_____

_____

_____

_____

_____

_____

The Creator who created all the earthly beauty we enjoy is the
same Creator who has prepared our heavenly home.
—ANNE GRAHAM LOTZ

_____

133

JULY

Thursday
9

Exalt the LORD our God, And worship at His footstool—He is holy.
Psalm 99:5

_____

_____

_____

_____

_____

_____

It is the essence of love to make itself heard.
—FREDERICK BUECHNER

Friday
10

But You, O LORD, are a shield for me,
My glory and the One who lifts up my head.
Psalm 3:3

_____

_____

_____

_____

_____

We want answers to our questions because sometimes they are easier to trust than God.
—BETH BOORAM

I will instruct you and teach you in the way you should go; I will guide you with My eye.
Psalm 32:8

What Christ asks us to do as His followers is to concentrate on keeping close to Him.
—PHILLIP KELLER

Everyone who loves is born of God and knows God.
1 John 4:7b

God's priority is that His love would become the hallmark of your life.
—BILLY GRAHAM

JULY

Monday
13

If anyone does not stumble in word, he is a perfect man, able also to bridle the whole body.
James 3:2b

_____

_____

_____

_____

_____

_____

Words are like nails driven into a wall. Even though you remove the nail, the hole remains.
—ROBERT JEFFRESS

Tuesday
14

Finally, all of you be of one mind, having compassion for one another; love as brothers, be tenderhearted, be courteous.
1 Peter 3:8

_____

_____

_____

_____

_____

_____

Success in marriage is more than finding the right person; it is being the right person.
—ROBERT BROWNING

JULY

My voice You shall hear in the morning, O LORD.
Psalm 5:3a

15

Prayer should be the key of the morning and the bolt of the night.
—HENRY GARIEPY

Thursday

You knit me together in my mother's womb.
Psalm 139:13b NIV

16

God placed his hand on the shoulder of humanity
and said, "You're something special."
—MAX LUCADO

JULY

Friday

17

When you do good and suffer, if you take it patiently,
this is commendable before God.
1 Peter 2:20b

We are never closer to God than when trials come upon us.
—CHARLES R. SWINDOLL

Saturday

18

I will cry out to God Most High,
To God who performs all things for me.
Psalm 57:2

God doesn't always do what we want Him to—but He
knows what's best for us, and He can be trusted.
—BILLY GRAHAM

JULY

Love never fails.
1 Corinthians 13:8a

_____

_____

_____

_____

_____

_____

_____

The major myth about love and a love relationship is
that it always looks pretty and feels good.
—JAN SILVIOUS

The humble He guides in justice,
And the humble He teaches His way.
Psalm 25:9

Monday

20

_____

_____

_____

_____

_____

_____

_____

Pride is self-absorption whether we're absorbed with
how miserable we are or how wonderful we are.
—BETH MOORE

JULY

Tuesday
21

For who is God, except the LORD? And who is a rock, except our God?
Psalm 18:31

_____

_____

_____

_____

_____

_____

When we rest in the very situation where God has lovingly placed us, we find the fabulous freedom of following.
—JENNIFER ROTHSCHILD

Wednesday
22

Behold what manner of love the Father has bestowed on us, that we should be called children of God!
1 John 3:1a

_____

_____

_____

_____

_____

_____

Life in Christ permits us to love others just as they are, no matter their status, race, or religion.
—LUCI SWINDOLL

JULY

A wholesome tongue is a tree of life.
Proverbs 15:4a

Offer your words like gifts that, when
unwrapped, bring grace to the hearer.
—PATSY CLAIRMONT

As the Father loved Me, I also have
loved you; abide in My love.
John 15:9

The great central terms of life in Christ are
faith, *hope*, *love*, and *peace*.
—DALLAS WILLARD

JULY

Saturday

25

Be an example to the believers in word, in conduct in love, in spirit, in faith, in purity.
1 Timothy 4:12b

Prayer proves its power by producing changes in us the pray-ers.
—PHILIP YANCEY

Sunday

26

We are hard-pressed on every side, yet not crushed; we are perplexed, but not in despair.
2 Corinthians 4:8

We cannot change our past, but we can learn to see our past from God's perspective.
—CHARLES R. SWINDOLL

JULY

Love one another fervently with a pure heart.
1 Peter 1:22b

If you see someone without a smile, give them one of yours.
—RICHARD DE HAAN

But the Helper, the Holy Spirit . . . will teach you all things
and bring to your remembrance all things that I said to you.
John 14:26

Getting to know God in all the ways that are
possible is a lifelong journey.
—HENRY CLOUD & JOHN TOWNSEND

143

JULY

Wednesday

29

And a wise man's heart discerns both time and judgment.
Ecclesiastes 8:5b

Make common sense your best friend.
Take it with you wherever you go.
—BRUCE BICKEL & STAN JANTZ

Thursday

30

Your word I have hidden in my heart,
That I might not sin against You.
Psalm 119:11

The Bible, like a bank, is most helpful when it's open.
—DAVID EGNER

JULY

Who is mighty like You, O LORD? Your
faithfulness also surrounds You.
Psalm 89:8

You and I can control nothing; God controls everything.

—JAN SILVIOUS

AUGUST 2009

MONDAY	TUESDAY	WEDNESDAY
3	4	5
Civic Holiday (Can.)		
10	11	12
17	18	19
24	25	26
31		
Late Summer Holiday (UK)		

THURSDAY	FRIDAY	SATURDAY/SUNDAY
		1
		2
6	7	8
		9
13	14	15 ASSUMPTION (BELG., FR., IT., SP., SWITZ.)
		16
20	21	22
		23
27	28	29
		30

True wisdom always leads us to please God.

—ANTHONY DESTEFANO

AUGUST

AUGUST

Saturday

1

Make me walk in the path of Your commandments,
For I delight in it.
Proverbs 119:35

Holiness is not a plateau we arrive at; it is a journey we embark on.
—JAN WINEBRENNER

Sunday

2

Hold fast the pattern of sound words which you have heard
from me, in faith and love, which are in Christ Jesus.
2 Timothy 1:13

The Christian faith is not true because it works.
It works because it is true.
—OS GUINNESS

AUGUST

Pursue righteousness, faith, love, peace with
those who call on the Lord out of a pure heart.
2 Timothy 2:22b

The truly courageous person is the one who is ready to sacrifice
his desires for the sake of something greater.
—ANTHONY DESTEFANO

Hear my prayer, O LORD, give ear
to my supplications!
Psalm 143:1a

We have to pray with our eyes on God, not on the difficulty.
—OSWALD CHAMBERS

AUGUST

Wednesday

5

All things were created through Him and for Him.
Colossians 1:16b

God loves each of us as if there were only one of us.
—ST. AUGUSTINE

Thursday

6

Present your bodies a living sacrifice,
holy, acceptable to God, which is your reasonable service.
Romans 12:1b

We can truly offer ourselves to God only if we
are willing to give up ourselves.
—MARVA DAWN

AUGUST

The LORD is good; His mercy is everlasting,
And His truth endures to all generations.
Psalm 100:5

Whatever is going on in my life, whether good or painful, is part of
a larger story that reaches from eternity to eternity.
—JAN WINEBRENNER

The righteous cry out, and the LORD hears,
And delivers them out of all their troubles.
Psalm 34:17

God is our rest and refuge right in the thick of our situation.
—MARK BUCHANAN

AUGUST

Sunday

9

If I say, "My foot slips," Your mercy,
O Lord, will hold me up.
Psalm 94:18

God loves you dearly, and the fact that you've been foolish
doesn't diminish His love one single ounce.
—BETH MOORE

Monday

10

He who walks in his uprightness fears the Lord.
Proverbs 14:2a

When no one else is interested in our capabilities and dreams,
God is still shouting His love over us.
—ALICIA BRITT CHOLE

AUGUST

Husbands, love your wives, just as Christ also
loved the church and gave Himself for her.
Ephesians 5:25

11

Great marriages always start with husbands
who learn how to love sacrificially.
—NEIL CLARK WARREN

Beloved, if God so loved us, we also
ought to love one another.
1 John 4:11

Wednesday

12

Because I am loved by God, and *only* because
of God's love, I can love others.
—LEONARD SWEET

AUGUST

Thursday

13

[Cast] all your care upon Him, for He cares for you.
1 Peter 5:7

Once we realize God holds us in His loving hands,
we can meet life's uncertainties with confidence.
—BILLY GRAHAM

Friday

14

The children of men put their trust under
the shadow of Your wings.
Psalm 36:7b

Surely we can trust God's ability to decide how
best to answer our prayers.
—LEITH ANDERSON

AUGUST

Keep your heart with all diligence,
For out of it spring the issues of life.
Proverbs 4:23

Without regular cleansing, the conscience slowly
becomes clogged and dirty.
—JEFF O'LEARY

O LORD, You are my God. I will exalt You,
I will praise Your name.
Isaiah 25:1a

Take God seriously, but don't take yourself too seriously.
—CHARLES R. SWINDOLL

AUGUST

Monday

17

Let my prayer come before You;
Incline Your ear to my cry.
Psalm 88:2

_____

_____

_____

_____

_____

_____

The book of Psalms is a ready-made prayer book.
—PHILIP YANCEY

Tuesday

18

Behold, I send My messenger,
And he will prepare the way before Me.
Malachi 3:1a

_____

_____

_____

_____

_____

God has no limit when it comes to solutions.
He can and will make a way.
—HENRY CLOUD & JOHN TOWNSEND

AUGUST

And walk in love, as Christ also has loved us
and given Himself for us.
Ephesians 5:2a

Wednesday

19

Every time we love, we demonstrate our obedience to Jesus Christ.
—LEITH ANDERSON

For You have made him most blessed forever.
Psalm 21:6a

Thursday

20

Jesus always has been, always is, always will be.
—ANNE GRAHAM LOTZ

AUGUST

Friday

21

And you are complete in Him, who is the head of all principality and power.
Colossians 2:10

_____

_____

_____

_____

_____

_____

Whatever salary you draw, your recompense
will be ultimately from Christ.
—FREDERICK BUECHNER

Saturday

22

I am the vine, you are the branches. He who abides in Me, and I in him, bears much fruit.
John 15:5a

_____

_____

_____

_____

_____

_____

God's longing to be with us speaks of His regard for us.
—BETH BOORAM

AUGUST

Create in me a clean heart, O God,
And renew a steadfast spirit within me.
Psalm 51:10

_____

_____

_____

_____

_____

_____

Character is not born. Character is formed.
—JEFF O'LEARY

Now we have received, not the spirit of the world,
but the Spirit who is from God.
1 Corinthians 2:12a

_____

_____

_____

_____

_____

We can't become like Christ on our own; we need God's help.
—BILLY GRAHAM

_____

AUGUST

Tuesday

25

I have chosen the way of truth.
Psalm 119:30a

_____

_____

_____

_____

_____

People who are set free from the shackles of
personal pride enjoy carefree abandon.
—PHILLIP KELLER

Wednesday

26

I will both lie down in peace, and sleep;
For You alone, O LORD, make me dwell in safety.
Psalm 4:8

_____

_____

_____

_____

_____

When you can't sleep, don't count sheep. Talk to the Shepherd.
—HENRY GARIEPY

AUGUST

For God is not unjust to forget your
work and labor of love.
Hebrews 6:10a

_____

_____

_____

_____

_____

_____

Every journey is accomplished one step at a time.
—CHARLES R. SWINDOLL

When you pass through the waters,
I will be with you.
Isaiah 43:2a

_____

_____

_____

_____

_____

When you don't understand why, just trust God!
Trust His heart! Trust His purpose!
—ANNE GRAHAM LOTZ

AUGUST

Saturday

29

The work of righteousness will be peace, And the effect of righteousness, quietness and assurance forever.
Isaiah 32:17

If we are not at peace with God, no other kind
of true peace is possible.
—MARVA DAWN

Sunday

30

And the glory which You gave Me I have given them,
that they may be one just as We are one.
John 17:22

God's will is for us to become more and more like Christ.
It's that simple—and that complex.
—BILLY GRAHAM

AUGUST

*For you were bought at a price; therefore glorify God in
your body and in your spirit, which are God's.*
1 Corinthians 6:20

When you follow the guidance of the Holy Spirit,
your life moves in the right direction.
—NEIL CLARK WARREN

SEPTEMBER 2009

MONDAY	TUESDAY	WEDNESDAY
	1	2
7	8	9
LABOR DAY (U.S., CAN.)		
14	15	16
		INDEPENDENCE DAY (MEX.)
21	22	23
	FALL BEGINS	
28	29	30
YOM KIPPUR		

THURSDAY	FRIDAY	SATURDAY/SUNDAY
3	4	5
		6
10	11	12
		13
	Patriot Day	Grandparent's Day
17	18	19
		Rosh Hashanah
		20
24	25	26
		27

Life is the total sum of what you do with the moments given you.

—ERWIN MCMANUS

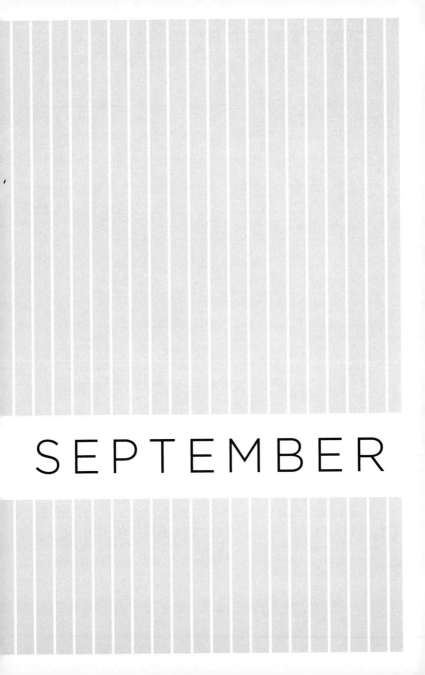

SEPTEMBER

SEPTEMBER

Tuesday

1

Whatever you do, do all to the glory of God.
1 Corinthians 10:31b

Diligence is not easy, but we can't reach our goals without it.
—HENRY CLOUD & JOHN TOWNSEND

Wednesday

2

For He performs what is appointed for me.
Job 23:14a

All our worry can accomplish absolutely nothing. But all our
praying entreats God to accomplish anything.
—BETH MOORE

SEPTEMBER

*Let the senior among you become like the junior; let the
leader act the part of the servant.*
Luke 22:26 MSG

3

Servant leaders accept more than their share of the
blame and less than their share of the credit.
—BRUCE BICKEL & STAN JANTZ

Friday

My soul, wait silently for God alone.
Psalm 62:5a

4

Prayer means keeping company with God who is already present.
—PHILIP YANCEY

SEPTEMBER

Saturday
5

Commit your works to the LORD,
And your thoughts will be established.
Proverbs 16:3

_____

_____

_____

_____

_____

_____

Deposit only positive thoughts in your mind. Withdraw
only positive thoughts from your mind.
—ANONYMOUS

Sunday
6

Nevertheless, we, according to His promise, look for new
heavens and a new earth in which righteousness dwells.
2 Peter 3:13

_____

_____

_____

_____

_____

Everything is *not* going to get fixed and healed in
this lifetime—that's what Heaven is for.
—ANITA RENFROE

SEPTEMBER

*God will help you deal with whatever hard things
come up when the time comes.*
Matthew 6:34b MSG

Monday

7

It is God's *love* that arranges our tomorrows
and whatever they bring.
—CHARLES R. SWINDOLL

*Each one should use whatever gift he has received to serve
others, faithfully administering God's grace in its various forms.*
1 Peter 4:10 NIV

Tuesday

8

You offer a gift to society that no one else brings.
If you don't bring it, it won't be brought.
—MAX LUCADO

SEPTEMBER

Wednesday

9

Rejoice in the Lord always. Again I will say, rejoice!
Philippians 4:4

A cheerful spirit is the flavoring in our soup;
without it the Christian life is bland.
—MIKE MASON

Thursday

10

But let us who are of the day be sober, putting
on the breastplate of faith and love.
1 Thessalonians 5:8a

Each day is ours to invest or to waste.
—HENRY GARIEPY

SEPTEMBER

Teach me Your way, O Lord,
And lead me in a smooth path.
Psalm 27:11a

Friday

11

What God desires most is that we walk with
Him humbly, quietly, and obediently.
—PHILLIP KELLER

Husbands, love your wives and
do not be bitter toward them.
Colossians 3:19

Saturday

12

Making your mate's happiness a priority not only brings him or her
happiness, but ensures a regret-free marriage for you.
—ROBERT JEFFRESS

SEPTEMBER

Sunday

13

He calls his own sheep by name
and leads them out.
John 10:3b

_____

_____

_____

_____

_____

_____

We are not nameless and faceless to God, but ones
He knows thoroughly and personally.
—BETH BOORAM

Monday

14

Teach me to do Your will,
For You are my God; Your Spirit is good.
Psalm 143:10a

_____

_____

_____

_____

_____

When we take responsibility for our lives
we're empowered to make changes.
—HENRY CLOUD & JOHN TOWNSEND

SEPTEMBER

The judgments of the LORD are true
and righteous altogether.
Psalm 19:9b

Tuesday
15

God gives the very best to those who leave the choice with Him.
—ELISABETH ELLIOT

You are My friends if you do
whatever I command you.
John 15:14

Wednesday
16

It is difficult to speak of loving our enemies when
we have a hard time just loving our friends.
—FREDERICK BUECHNER

SEPTEMBER

Thursday

17

Now therefore, listen to me, my children
For blessed are those who keep my ways.
Proverbs 8:32

_____

_____

_____

_____

_____

_____

Listening is an art, and I must learn to listen to God.
—PHILIP YANCEY

Friday

18

Be filled with the knowledge of His will in all
wisdom and spiritual understanding.
Colossians 1:9b

_____

_____

_____

_____

_____

_____

The Christian life is a journey—one that will
take us the rest of our lives.
—BILLY GRAHAM

SEPTEMBER

Jesus said to him, "I am the way, the truth, and the life. No one comes to the Father except through Me."
John 14:6

Saturday

19

God is equally available to all who come to Him.
—JEFF O'LEARY

He who dwells in the secret place of the Most High
Shall abide under the shadow of the Almighty.
Psalm 91:1

Sunday

20

The greatest good in life is to live for and to worship God.
—LEITH ANDERSON

SEPTEMBER

Monday

21

God is my strength and power,
And He makes my way perfect.
2 Samuel 22:33

Failure is the path of least persistence.
—BRUCE BICKEL & STAN JANTZ

Tuesday

22

But I trust in your unfailing love; my heart
rejoices in your salvation.
Psalm 13:5 NIV

We have to trust God's silences and wait for God's answers.
—ANNE GRAHAM LOTZ

SEPTEMBER

Behold, children are a heritage from the LORD,
The fruit of the womb is a reward.
Psalm 127:3

When we remember what a treasure our children are,
we will treat them with great dignity.
—NEIL CLARK WARREN

In everything give thanks; for this is the will
of God in Christ Jesus for you.
1 Thessalonians 5:18

If we believe our affairs are in God's hands, every event,
whether joyous or tragic, will be taken as part of His plan.
—PHILLIP KELLER

SEPTEMBER

Friday

25

Let another man praise you, and not your own mouth.
Proverbs 27:2a

_____

_____

_____

_____

_____

Don't worry when you are not recognized,
but strive to be worthy of recognition.
—ABRAHAM LINCOLN

Saturday

26

Surely goodness and mercy shall follow me all the days of my life.
Psalm 23:6a

_____

_____

_____

_____

Never fear that God is not at work while you wait.
He's doing what no one else can.
—BETH MOORE

SEPTEMBER

Six days you shall labor and do all your work, but the seventh day is the Sabbath of the LORD your God.
Exodus 20:9–10a

Sunday

27

All things made by God need rest—especially us.
—MARK BUCHANAN

God has poured out his love into our hearts by the Holy Spirit, whom he has given us.
Romans 5:5b NIV

Monday

28

God so loves you that your pain is His. Your tears are on His face!
—ANNE GRAHAM LOTZ

SEPTEMBER

Tuesday
29

In the fear of the LORD there is strong confidence.
Proverbs 14:26a

We create our own history, day by day,
decision by decision, habit by habit.
—JEFF O'LEARY

Wednesday
30

And I am convinced that nothing can ever
separate us from God's love.
Romans 8:38a, NLT

Nothing is stronger than God's love for you—nothing difficult,
nothing painful—nothing!
—JAN WINEBRENNER

PERSONAL NOTES

OCTOBER 2009

MONDAY	TUESDAY	WEDNESDAY
5	6	7
12	13	14
Columbus Day (U.S.) Thanksgiving Day (Can.)		
19	20	21
26	27	28
Labour Day (NZ)		

THURSDAY	FRIDAY	SATURDAY/SUNDAY
1	2	3
		4
		St. Francis Day
8	9	10
		11
15	16	17
		18
	Boss's Day (U.S.)	
22	23	24
		25
29	30	31
		Halloween

Whatever our situation in life—butcher, baker, candlestick maker— our deepest and most pressing need is to learn to walk with God.

—JOHN ELDREDGE

OCTOBER

OCTOBER

Thursday

1

*I have learned in whatever state
I am, to be content.
Philippians 4:11b*

To keep your life in perspective, keep all your stuff in perspective.
—BRUCE BICKEL & STAN JANTZ

Friday

2

*His lord said to him, "Well done, good and faithful servant."
Matthew 25:23a*

Heavenly wisdom can only be acquired
from the Greatest of Teachers.
—F. B. MEYER

OCTOBER

Wait on the LORD; Be of good courage,
And He shall strengthen your heart.
Psalm 27:14a

3

_____

_____

_____

_____

_____

_____

_____

Patience means waiting for God's time without doubting His love.
—DENNIS DE HAAN

Whoever loses his life for My sake and the
gospel's will save it.
Mark 8:35b

4

_____

_____

_____

_____

_____

We can do great things for God if we are
willing to do little things for others.
—DAVID EGNER

OCTOBER

Monday

5

*Every good gift and every perfect gift is from above,
and comes down from the Father of lights.*
James 1:17a

Who indeed deserves our praise but the God who
originated every good and perfect gift.
—PHILIP YANCEY

Tuesday

6

*Now thanks be to God who always leads
us in triumph in Christ.*
2 Corinthians 2:14a

When I can laugh about some part of a problem,
the whole situation suddenly seems less negative.
—MARILYN MEBERG

OCTOBER

*For I will set my eyes on them for good, and
I will bring them back to this land.*
Jeremiah 24:6a

7

God finds impossibly creative ways to convert our
liabilities into our best features.
—CAROLYN ARENDS

Thursday

See, I have engraved you on the palms of my hands.
Isaiah 49:16a NIV

8

We are not in the hands of blind fate! We are in the hands of God.
—CHARLES R. SWINDOLL

OCTOBER

Friday

9

I have made them for my glory.
It was I who created them.
Isaiah 43:7b NLT

_____

_____

_____

_____

_____

_____

You are the only you that God made.
—MAX LUCADO

Saturday

10

God is our refuge and strength.
Psalm 46:1a

_____

_____

_____

_____

_____

_____

God turns our sorrows into symphonies.
—HENRY GARIEPY

OCTOBER

Are not two sparrows sold for a copper coin? And not one
of them falls to the ground apart from your Father's will.
Matthew 10:29

If God keeps tabs on every sparrow, then surely
He keeps special tabs on you.
—JONI EARECKSON TADA

He who believes in Me, as the Scripture has said,
out of his heart will flow rivers of living water.
John 7:38

To sense and know God is to have tasted life at its sublime best.
—PHILLIP KELLER

OCTOBER

Tuesday
13

God is light and in Him is no darkness at all.
1 John 1:5b

When we muddle through a dark day we have the assurance that what is dark to us isn't dark to God at all.
—BETH BOORAM

Wednesday
14

If we live in the Spirit, let us also walk in the Spirit.
Galatians 5:25

We should not only want to be merciful and patient persons but should be making plans to become so.
—DALLAS WILLARD

OCTOBER

For you are great, and do wondrous things;
You alone are God.
Psalm 86:10

Thursday
15

It is God you shall love first before you love anything else.
—FREDERICK BUECHNER

Whatever your hand finds to do,
do it with your might.
Ecclesiastes 9:10a

Friday
16

When we see our work as something God gave us,
even the routine tasks take on significance.
—BILLY GRAHAM

OCTOBER

Saturday

17

Therefore, to him who knows to do good and does not do it, to him it is sin.
James 4:17

Good intentions are meaningless unless you put them into action.
—BRUCE BICKEL & STAN JANTZ

Sunday

18

So we may boldly say: "The Lord is my helper; I will not fear. What can man do to me?"
Hebrews 13:6

Jesus guarantees our direct access to God through Him!
—ANNE GRAHAM LOTZ

OCTOBER

I will run the course of Your commandments,
For You shall enlarge my heart.
Psalm 119:32

God has prepared a mighty work for your life, an
incredible significance for your days.
—JEFF O'LEARY

The Lord is on my side; I will not fear.
What can man do to me?
Psalm 118:6

Trust is complete confidence and dependence
upon God for the right outcome.
—LEITH ANDERSON

OCTOBER

21

For this reason a man shall leave his father and mother and be joined to his wife, and the two shall become one flesh.
Ephesians 5:31

Show me a marriage in which the in-laws meddle,
and I will show you a marriage in trouble.
—NEIL CLARK WARREN

Thursday

22

By humility and the fear of the LORD
Are riches and honor and life.
Proverbs 22:4

Christianity holds out the truth that an
ego trip is a journey to nowhere.
—LEONARD SWEET

OCTOBER

Behold, You desire truth in the inward parts,
And in the hidden part You will make me to know wisdom.
Psalm 51:6

The first place we need to look for wisdom
is directly from God Himself.
—HENRY CLOUD & JOHN TOWNSEND

But the path of the just is like the shining sun,
That shines ever brighter unto the perfect day.
Proverbs 4:18

Every choice we make is an investment in a future
we cannot see. Some invest wisely, some poorly.
—ALICIA BRITT CHOLE

OCTOBER

Sunday

25

The LORD is good to all,
And His tender mercies are over all His works.
Psalm 145:9

Because God is infinite, you will never reach
the end of all He offers of Himself.
—BETH MOORE

Monday

26

But He knows the way that I take;
When He has tested me, I shall come forth as gold.
Job 23:10

God is more interested in changing your thinking than
in changing your circumstances.
—MARK BUCHANAN

OCTOBER

But you, when you pray, . . . pray to your Father
who is in the secret place.
Matthew 6:6a

27

_____

_____

_____

_____

_____

_____

_____

Jesus taught three principles of prayer: keep it honest,
keep it simple, and keep it up.
—PHILIP YANCEY

Wednesday

And His kingdom is from generation to generation.
Daniel 4:34b

28

_____

_____

_____

_____

_____

_____

God's kingdom purposes will prevail, regardless
of the storms that encircle our world.
—JAN WINEBRENNER

OCTOBER

Thursday

29

The Spirit of God has made me,
And the breath of the Almighty gives me life.
Job 33:4

_____

_____

_____

_____

_____

Inside of you, God plants His dream for your life.
It's up to you to seek it, find it, and fulfill it.
—JEFF O'LEARY

Friday

30

For you have need of endurance, so that after you have
done the will of God, you may receive the promise.
Hebrews 10:36

_____

_____

_____

_____

_____

When we cast our burdens upon the Lord, they might
not go away, but we will be able to endure them.
—MARVA DAWN

OCTOBER

He shall cover you with His feathers,
And under His wings you shall take refuge.
Psalm 91:4a

When the first angel lifted the first wing,
God had already always been.
—MAX LUCADO

NOVEMBER 2009

MONDAY	TUESDAY	WEDNESDAY
2	3	4
	Election Day (U.S.)	
9	10	11
		Armistice Day (Belg., Fr.) Veteran's Day (U.S.) Remembrance Day (Can.)
16	17	18
23 30	24	25

THURSDAY	FRIDAY	SATURDAY/SUNDAY
		1 ALL SAINTS' DAY (BELG., FR., IT., SP., SWITZ.) ALL SOULS' DAY (MEX.)
5	6	7 / 8
12	13	14 / 15
19	20	21 / 22
26 THANKSGIVING DAY (U.S.)	27	28 / 29 ADVENT BEGINS

We can confidently
journey on our path
of life, knowing
that we have an
all-knowing, unerring,
and loving Guide.

—HENRY GARIEPY

NOVEMBER

NOVEMBER

Sunday

1

Now may the God of hope fill you with all joy and peace . . . that you may abound in hope.
Romans 15:13a

We are surrounded by a God who loves us supremely.
—JAN SILVIOUS

Monday

2

I have put my trust in the Lord GOD,
That I may declare all Your works.
Psalm 73:28b

The history of the world is really the history of God trying to communicate with mankind.
—ANTHONY DESTEFANO

NOVEMBER

Draw near to God and He will draw near to you.
James 4:8a

3

_____

_____

_____

_____

_____

_____

_____

Everything in our hearts that is less or other than
God must be smashed, for it is not God.
—OS GUINNESS

_____

Just as He chose us in Him . . . that we should be
holy and without blame before Him in love.
Ephesians 1:4

Wednesday

4

_____

_____

_____

_____

_____

_____

Holiness, not happiness, is the chief end of man.
—OSWALD CHAMBERS

_____

NOVEMBER

Peace I leave with you, My peace I give you. . . . Let not your heart be troubled, neither let it be afraid.
John 14:27

Faith in a prayer-hearing God will make a prayer-loving Christian.
—ANDREW MURRAY

Fulfill my joy by being like-minded, having the same love, being of one accord, of one mind.
Philippians 2:2

There is nothing that makes us love a man
so much as praying for him.
—WILLIAM LAW

NOVEMBER

Jesus said to him, "If you can believe, all things are possible to him who believes."
Mark 9:23

Prayer is not so much an act as an attitude—
an attitude of dependence on God.
—ARTHUR PINK

Holy Father, keep through Your name those whom You have given Me, that they may be one as We are.
John 17:11b

As we grow in the Christian faith and life, we are
always becoming who we are meant to be.
—MARVA DAWN

NOVEMBER

Monday

9

In this is love, not that we loved God, but that He loved us and sent His Son to be the propitiation for our sins.
1 John 4:10

_____

_____

_____

_____

_____

_____

In the unfathomable horror of the cross, lay the inconceivable depths of God's love.
—JAN WINEBRENNER

Tuesday

10

The labor of the righteous leads to life.
Proverbs 10:16a

_____

_____

_____

_____

_____

_____

There is sanctity in honest work. It pleases the heart of God.
—MARK BUCHANAN

NOVEMBER

An excellent wife is the crown of her husband.
Proverbs 12:4a

Wednesday

11

If you honor your husband every chance you have, you will
contribute to his becoming a husband you will always admire.
—NEIL CLARK WARREN

For the LORD God is a sun and shield;
The LORD will give grace and glory.
Psalm 84:11a

Thursday

12

Trusting God is believing that He is good and wise even
when we cannot explain all that is going on.
—LEITH ANDERSON

NOVEMBER

Friday
13

Let the word of Christ dwell in you
richly in all wisdom.
Colossians 3:16a

_____

_____

_____

_____

_____

Whatever good I can do, I must be diligent about finishing it.
—JEFF O'LEARY

Saturday
14

He has put a new song in my mouth—
Praise to our God.
Psalm 40:3a

_____

_____

_____

_____

_____

It doesn't matter whether you have a beautiful voice or make
mostly noise, you were born for song—a God-song.
—BETH MOORE

NOVEMBER

*We know that when He is revealed we shall be
like Him, for we shall see Him as He is.*
1 John 3:2

We should never live out in our thoughts what we
know we should not live out in our lives.
—ALICIA BRITT CHOLE

---

*Search me, O God, and know my heart; . . . And
lead me in the way everlasting.*
Psalm 139:23–24

We can confidently seek God's will,
knowing it is always best for us—always.
—BILLY GRAHAM

NOVEMBER

Tuesday

17

And in the night His song shall be with me—
a prayer to the God of my life.
Psalm 42:8b

God is the Composer of the music of the night,
music that sets us free from the darkness.
—HENRY GARIEPY

Wednesday

18

I will greatly rejoice in the LORD,
My soul shall be joyful in my God.
Isaiah 61:10a

Any of our days God touches are transformed with
the light and joy of His presence.
—PHILLIP KELLER

NOVEMBER

Great is Your faithfulness.
Lamentations 3:23b

19

As soon as we finish praising God for one thing,
He gives us something else.
—THELMA WELLS

And He is before all things, and in Him all things consist.
Colossians 1:17

20

Of all we don't know about the creation, there is
one thing we do know—God did it with a smile.
—MAX LUCADO

NOVEMBER

Saturday

21

God is love, and he who abides in love abides in God, and God in him.
1 John 4:16b

_____

_____

_____

_____

_____

_____

As you and I are filled with God, we will be filled with His love.
—ANNE GRAHAM LOTZ

Sunday

22

In due season we shall reap if we do not lose heart.
Galatians 6:9b

_____

_____

_____

_____

_____

_____

Prayer means opening myself to God and not limiting
Him through my own preconceptions.
—PHILIP YANCEY

NOVEMBER

Do not be overcome by evil, but
overcome evil with good.
Romans 12:21

Monday

23

We can be sure, when we are God's, that even in the
midst of turmoil we can experience good.
—MARVA DAWN

When you pass through the waters,
I will be with you.
Isaiah 43:2a

Tuesday

24

We have to accept the reality that God's love
does not shield us from loss and hardship.
—BETH BOORAM

NOVEMBER

Wednesday

25

For God has not given us a spirit of fear,
but of power and of love and of a sound mind.
2 Timothy 1:7

We are designed to flourish when we connect to and love God.
—HENRY CLOUD & JOHN TOWNSEND

Thursday

26

I press on, that I may lay hold of that for which Christ
Jesus has also laid hold of me.
Philippians 3:12b

Great works are performed not by strength but by perseverance.
—SAMUEL JOHNSON

NOVEMBER

Blessed is the man whom You instruct,
O LORD, and teach out of Your law.
Psalm 94:12

What goes into your mind and heart comes out in your life.
—BRUCE BICKEL & STAN JANTZ

For we are His workmanship, created in
Christ Jesus for good works.
Ephesians 2:10

When I allow God to govern my life, I am set free
from the tyranny of self-centeredness.
—PHILLIP KELLER

NOVEMBER

Sunday

29

If we confess our sins, he is faithful and just and will forgive us our sins and purify us from all unrighteousness.
1 John 1:9 NIV

The only sin God cannot forgive is the sin of refusing His forgiveness.
—BILLY GRAHAM

Monday

30

Always pursue what is good both for yourselves and for all.
1 Thessalonians 5:15b

Things can be replaced. What we can't replace are people and relationships.
—BRUCE BICKEL & STAN JANTZ

PERSONAL NOTES

DECEMBER 2009

MONDAY	TUESDAY	WEDNESDAY
	1	2
7	8 IMMACULATE CONCEPTION (IT., SP., SWITZ.)	9
14	15	16
21 WINTER BEGINS	22	23
28	29	30

THURSDAY	FRIDAY	SATURDAY/SUNDAY
3	4	5
		6
10	11	12
		HANUKKAH
		13
17	18	19
		20
24	25	26
		BOXING DAY (AUST., CAN., UK, NZ)
		ST. STEPHEN'S DAY (SP.)
		27
CHRISTMAS EVE	CHRISTMAS	
31		
NEW YEAR'S EVE		

What keeps the wild hope of Christmas alive is the haunting dream that the child who was born that day may yet be born again even in us.

—FREDERICK BUECHNER

DECEMBER

DECEMBER

Tuesday

1

Live in peace; and the God of love and peace will be with you.
2 Corinthians 13:11b

_____

_____

_____

_____

_____

_____

God and peace are inseparable. If you try to obtain one without the other, you're doomed to failure.
—ANTHONY DESTEFANO

Wednesday

2

And you who seek God, your hearts shall live.
Psalm 69:32b

_____

_____

_____

_____

_____

_____

God is never in a hurry.
—OSWALD CHAMBERS

DECEMBER

Then I will give them a heart to know Me,
that I am the LORD.
Jeremiah 24:7a

Thursday

3

We need never shout across the spaces to an absent God.
He is nearer than our own soul.
—A. W. TOZER

So then faith comes by hearing,
and hearing by the word of God.
Romans 10:17

Friday

4

Faith is believing what you do not see; the reward
of faith is to see what you believe.
—ST. AUGUSTINE

DECEMBER

Saturday

5

My times are in Your hand.
Psalm 31:15a

_____

_____

_____

_____

_____

_____

God gives us the perfect freedom to be wholly ourselves,
under His wise and loving care.
—MARVA DAWN

Sunday

6

You are good, and do good;
Teach me Your statutes.
Psalm 119:68

_____

_____

_____

_____

_____

We insist on defining what we think God's love should
look like and how He should deal with us.
—JAN WINEBRENNER

DECEMBER

Be thankful to Him, and bless His name.
For the LORD is good.
Psalm 100:4b–5a

To give thanks in all circumstances, for all things,
is a declaration of God's sovereign goodness.
—MARK BUCHANAN

The LORD searches all hearts and understands
all the intent of the thoughts. . . .
1 Chronicles 28:9b

God looks not only at what we've done and how,
but also at why we did it.
—BETH MOORE

DECEMBER

Wednesday

9

I will wait for You, O You his Strength:
For God is my defense.
Psalm 59:9

God stands beside us faithfully while we pray,
while we wait, and while we weep.
—ALICIA BRITT CHOLE

Thursday

10

[Love] does not behave rudely, does not
seek its own, is not provoked.
1 Corinthians 13:5

Love shouldn't be given or taken away because of behavior,
performance, or any other component.
—NEIL CLARK WARREN

DECEMBER

*If you abide in Me, and My words abide in you, you will
ask what you desire, and it shall be done for you.*
John 15:7

Jesus was good, loving, kind, compassionate; so we
should be good, loving, kind, compassionate.
—JAMES SIRE

*He does great things which
we cannot comprehend.*
Job 37:5b

When you take on a God-sized challenge,
self-sufficiency is no longer an option.
—ERWIN MCMANUS

DECEMBER

Sunday

13

We have this treasure in earthen vessels, that the excellence of the power may be of God and not of us.
2 Corinthians 4:7

God created me to be myself—formed in His image—nothing more nor less.
—MIKE MASON

Monday

14

But grow in the grace and knowledge of our Lord and Savior Jesus Christ.
2 Peter 3:18a

Develop a fierce and tenacious concentration upon your God-given destiny.
—JEFF O'LEARY

DECEMBER

Love your enemies, do good to those who hate you.
Luke 6:27b

15

God speaks of love as being a choice we make.
It is choosing to care for others.
—LEITH ANDERSON

To everything there is a season: . . . a time
to weep, . . . a time to mourn.
Ecclesiastes 3:1, 4

Wednesday

16

Grieving is acknowledging the pain in our hearts
and letting God in as we do.
—BETH BOORAM

DECEMBER

Thursday

17

Lead me in Your truth and teach me,
For You are the God of my salvation.
Psalm 25:5a

God doesn't cram His will down our throats. But we know that it always turns out to be the best for us.
—MARVA DAWN

Friday

18

Your rod and Your staff, they comfort me.
Psalm 23:4b

When we are sorrowful, God comforts; when we are weak, He strengthens.
—HENRY GARIEPY

DECEMBER

*For it is God who works in you both to will and
to do for His good pleasure.*
Philippians 2:13

Whether you work at home or in the marketplace,
your work matters to God.
—MAX LUCADO

*And we know that all things work together for
good to those who love God.*
Romans 8:28a

All the earthly struggles that occur are not accidents.
God is in the midst of them.
—CHARLES R. SWINDOLL

DECEMBER

Monday
21

In Him we have redemption through his blood, the forgiveness of sins, according to the riches of His grace.
Ephesians 1:7

_____

_____

_____

_____

_____

_____

Forgiveness is our deliberate willingness to let something go—letting it go to God.
—BETH MOORE

Tuesday
22

The testing of your faith produces patience.
James 1:3b

_____

_____

_____

_____

_____

_____

Everyone who keeps company with God goes through bright, joyful times as well as dark, wintry times.
—PHILIP YANCEY

DECEMBER

*And David said to his son Solomon, "Be strong
and of good courage, and do it."
1 Chronicles 28:20a*

Success is not the destination; it is the daily progress
you make in small steps toward the destination.
—BRUCE BICKEL & STAN JANTZ

*Forgive as the Lord forgave you.
Colossians 3:13b NIV*

God forgave us freely and fully, and that's how we
are to forgive others: freely and fully.
—BILLY GRAHAM

DECEMBER

Friday

25

For the Son of Man will come in the glory of His Father.
Matthew 16:27a

Jesus is fully present in every age, every
generation, every culture, every nation.
—ANNE GRAHAM LOTZ

Saturday

26

And God is able to make all grace abound toward you.
2 Corinthians 9:8a

A life touched by God always ends in touching others.
—ERWIN MCMANUS

DECEMBER

And we know that the Son of God has come and has
given us an understanding.
1 John 5:20a

Always assume the best about others and
it will be easy to show them respect.
—ANONYMOUS

Like an apple tree among the trees of the woods,
so is my beloved among the sons.
Song of Solomon 2:3a

If a man knows his wife believes in him, he is empowered
to do better in every area of life.
—SHAUNTI FELDHAHN

DECEMBER

Tuesday

29

Children, obey your parents in the Lord, for this is right.
Ephesians 6:1

_____

_____

_____

_____

_____

Any family that frequently and enthusiastically honors the mother and father has tremendous potential.
—NEIL CLARK WARREN

Wednesday

30

For this reason I bow my knees to the Father of our Lord Jesus Christ.
Ephesians 3:14

_____

_____

_____

_____

_____

We increase our ability, stability, and responsibility when we increase our sense of accountability to God.
—BRUCE BICKEL & STAN JANTZ

DECEMBER

You will show me the path of life;
In Your presence is fullness of joy.
Psalm 16:11a

We can commune with God anywhere
along the winding trails of life.
—PHILLIP KELLER

NOTES FOR 2010

January

February

March

April

May

June

NOTES FOR 2010

July
_____
_____
_____
_____
_____

August
_____
_____
_____
_____

September
_____
_____
_____
_____

October
_____
_____
_____
_____

November
_____
_____
_____
_____

December
_____
_____
_____
_____
_____

2009

January

S	M	T	W	T	F	S
				1	2	3
4	5	6	7	8	9	10
11	12	13	14	15	16	17
18	19	20	21	22	23	24
25	26	27	28	29	30	31

May

S	M	T	W	T	F	S
					1	2
3	4	5	6	7	8	9
10	11	12	13	14	15	16
17	18	19	20	21	22	23
24	25	26	27	28	29	30
31						

September

S	M	T	W	T	F	S
		1	2	3	4	5
6	7	8	9	10	11	12
13	14	15	16	17	18	19
20	21	22	23	24	25	26
27	28	29	30			

February

S	M	T	W	T	F	S
1	2	3	4	5	6	7
8	9	10	11	12	13	14
15	16	17	18	19	20	21
22	23	24	25	26	27	28

June

S	M	T	W	T	F	S
	1	2	3	4	5	6
7	8	9	10	11	12	13
14	15	16	17	18	19	20
21	22	23	24	25	26	27
28	29	30				

October

S	M	T	W	T	F	S
				1	2	3
4	5	6	7	8	9	10
11	12	13	14	15	16	17
18	19	20	21	22	23	24
25	26	27	28	29	30	31

March

S	M	T	W	T	F	S
1	2	3	4	5	6	7
8	9	10	11	12	13	14
15	16	17	18	19	20	21
22	23	24	25	26	27	28
29	30	31				

July

S	M	T	W	T	F	S
			1	2	3	4
5	6	7	8	9	10	11
12	13	14	15	16	17	18
19	20	21	22	23	24	25
26	27	28	29	30	31	

November

S	M	T	W	T	F	S
1	2	3	4	5	6	7
8	9	10	11	12	13	14
15	16	17	18	19	20	21
22	23	24	25	26	27	28
29	30					

April

S	M	T	W	T	F	S
			1	2	3	4
5	6	7	8	9	10	11
12	13	14	15	16	17	18
19	20	21	22	23	24	25
26	27	28	29	30		

August

S	M	T	W	T	F	S
						1
2	3	4	5	6	7	8
9	10	11	12	13	14	15
16	17	18	19	20	21	22
23	24	25	26	27	28	29
30	31					

December

S	M	T	W	T	F	S
		1	2	3	4	5
6	7	8	9	10	11	12
13	14	15	16	17	18	19
20	21	22	23	24	25	26
27	28	29	30	31		

2010

January

S	M	T	W	T	F	S
					1	2
3	4	5	6	7	8	9
10	11	12	13	14	15	16
17	18	19	20	21	22	23
24	25	26	27	28	29	30
31						

February

S	M	T	W	T	F	S
	1	2	3	4	5	6
7	8	9	10	11	12	13
14	15	16	17	18	19	20
21	22	23	24	25	26	27
28						

March

S	M	T	W	T	F	S
	1	2	3	4	5	6
7	8	9	10	11	12	13
14	15	16	17	18	19	20
21	22	23	24	25	26	27
28	29	30	31			

April

S	M	T	W	T	F	S
				1	2	3
4	5	6	7	8	9	10
11	12	13	14	15	16	17
18	19	20	21	22	23	24
25	26	27	28	29	30	

May

S	M	T	W	T	F	S
						1
2	3	4	5	6	7	8
9	10	11	12	13	14	15
16	17	18	19	20	21	22
23	24	25	26	27	28	29
30	31					

June

S	M	T	W	T	F	S
		1	2	3	4	5
6	7	8	9	10	11	12
13	14	15	16	17	18	19
20	21	22	23	24	25	26
27	28	29	30			

July

S	M	T	W	T	F	S
				1	2	3
4	5	6	7	8	9	10
11	12	13	14	15	16	17
18	19	20	21	22	23	24
25	26	27	28	29	30	31

August

S	M	T	W	T	F	S
1	2	3	4	5	6	7
8	9	10	11	12	13	14
15	16	17	18	19	20	21
22	23	24	25	26	27	28
29	30	31				

September

S	M	T	W	T	F	S
			1	2	3	4
5	6	7	8	9	10	11
12	13	14	15	16	17	18
19	20	21	22	23	24	25
26	27	28	29	30		

October

S	M	T	W	T	F	S
					1	2
3	4	5	6	7	8	9
10	11	12	13	14	15	16
17	18	19	20	21	22	23
24	25	26	27	28	29	30
31						

November

S	M	T	W	T	F	S
	1	2	3	4	5	6
7	8	9	10	11	12	13
14	15	16	17	18	19	20
21	22	23	24	25	26	27
28	29	30				

December

S	M	T	W	T	F	S
			1	2	3	4
5	6	7	8	9	10	11
12	13	14	15	16	17	18
19	20	21	22	23	24	25
26	27	28	29	30	31	

2011

January

S	M	T	W	T	F	S
						1
2	3	4	5	6	7	8
9	10	11	12	13	14	15
16	17	18	19	20	21	22
23	24	25	26	27	28	29
30	31					

February

S	M	T	W	T	F	S
		1	2	3	4	5
6	7	8	9	10	11	12
13	14	15	16	17	18	19
20	21	22	23	24	25	26
27	28					

March

S	M	T	W	T	F	S
		1	2	3	4	5
6	7	8	9	10	11	12
13	14	15	16	17	18	19
20	21	22	23	24	25	26
27	28	29	30	31		

April

S	M	T	W	T	F	S
					1	2
3	4	5	6	7	8	9
10	11	12	13	14	15	16
17	18	19	20	21	22	23
24	25	26	27	28	29	30

May

S	M	T	W	T	F	S
1	2	3	4	5	6	7
8	9	10	11	12	13	14
15	16	17	18	19	20	21
22	23	24	25	26	27	28
29	30	31				

June

S	M	T	W	T	F	S
			1	2	3	4
5	6	7	8	9	10	11
12	13	14	15	16	17	18
19	20	21	22	23	24	25
26	27	28	29	30		

July

S	M	T	W	T	F	S
					1	2
3	4	5	6	7	8	9
10	11	12	13	14	15	16
17	18	19	20	21	22	23
24	25	26	27	28	29	30
31						

August

S	M	T	W	T	F	S
	1	2	3	4	5	6
7	8	9	10	11	12	13
14	15	16	17	18	19	20
21	22	23	24	25	26	27
28	29	30	31			

September

S	M	T	W	T	F	S
				1	2	3
4	5	6	7	8	9	10
11	12	13	14	15	16	17
18	19	20	21	22	23	24
25	26	27	28	29	30	

October

S	M	T	W	T	F	S
						1
2	3	4	5	6	7	8
9	10	11	12	13	14	15
16	17	18	19	20	21	22
23	24	25	26	27	28	29
30	31					

November

S	M	T	W	T	F	S
		1	2	3	4	5
6	7	8	9	10	11	12
13	14	15	16	17	18	19
20	21	22	23	24	25	26
27	28	29	30			

December

S	M	T	W	T	F	S
				1	2	3
4	5	6	7	8	9	10
11	12	13	14	15	16	17
18	19	20	21	22	23	24
25	26	27	28	29	30	31

Important Telephone Numbers

Name	Telephone
Name	Telephone
Name	Telephone
Name	Telephone
Name	Telephone
Name	Telephone
Name	Telephone
Name	Telephone
Name	Telephone
Name	Telephone
Name	Telephone
Name	Telephone
Name	Telephone
Name	Telephone
Name	Telephone
Name	Telephone
Name	Telephone
Name	Telephone
Name	Telephone
Name	Telephone
Name	Telephone
Name	Telephone
Name	Telephone
Name	Telephone
Name	Telephone
Name	Telephone
Name	Telephone
Name	Telephone

Toll-Free Telephone Numbers

Hotels

Best Western 800-780-7234
Choice Hotels 877-424-6423
Doubletree 800-222-8733
Fairmont Hotels 800-257-7544
Hampton Inns 800-426-7866
Hilton 800-445-8667
Holiday Inns 888-890-0242
Hyatt Hotels 888-591-1234
InterContinental . . .800-424-6835
Marriott Hotels 888-236-2427
Omni Hotels 888-444-6664
Radisson 888-201-1718
Ramada Inns 800-272-6232
Sheraton Hotels 800-325-3535
Travelodge 800-578-7878
Westin 800-598-1864

Car Rentals

Alamo 800-462-5266
Avis 800-331-1212
Budget 800-527-7000
Dollar 800-800-4000
Hertz 800-654-3131
National 800-227-7368
Thrifty 800-847-4389

Credit Cards

American Express 800-528-4800
Diners Club 800-234-6377
Discover 800-347-2683
Master Card 800-627-8372
Visa 800-847-2911

Airlines

Air Canada 888-247-2262
Air Mexico 800-237-6639
American 800-433-7300
America West 800-428-4322
British Airways 800-247-9297
Continental 800-523-3273
Delta 800-221-1212
Frontier 800-432-1359
Japan Airlines 800-525-3663
Northwest/KLM 800-225-2525
Southwest 800-435-9792
United 800-864-8331

Courier Services

DHL Airlines 800-225-5345
Federal Express 800-463-3339
UPS 800-742-5877

International Country Codes

Algeria	213	Kuwait	965
Argentina	54	Lebanon	961
Australia	61	Libya, Arab People's Soc. Jam.	218
Austria	43	Luxembourg	352
Bangladesh	880	Malaysia	60
Belgium	32	Malta	356
Bolivia	591	Mexico	52
Brazil	55	Monaco	377
Bulgaria	359	Morocco	212
Chile	56	Nepal	977
China, People's Rep of	86	Netherlands	31
CIS—Russia	7	New Zealand	64
Colombia	57	Nicaragua	505
Cyprus	357	Nigeria, Fed Rep of	234
The Czech Rep, Slovakia	420	Norway	47
Denmark	45	Pakistan	92
Ecuador	593	Panama	507
Egypt, Arab Rep of	20	Paraguay	595
El Salvador	503	Peru	51
Ethiopia	251	Philippines	63
Fiji Islands	679	Poland, Rep of	48
Finland	358	Portugal	351
France	33	Romania	40
Germany, Fed Rep of	49	Samoa [American]	684
Ghana	233	Saudi Arabia	966
Gibraltar	350	Singapore	65
Greece	30	South Africa, Rep of	27
Guatemala	502	Spain	34
Honduras	504	Sri Lanka, Dem. Soc. Rep of	94
Hong Kong	852	Sudan	249
Hungary	36	Swaziland	268
Iceland	354	Sweden	46
India	91	Switzerland	41
Indonesia	62	Taiwan, Rep of China	886
Iran	98	Thailand	66
Iraq	964	Tunisia	216
Ireland, Rep of	353	Turkey	90
Israel	972	United Arab Emirates	971
Italy	39	United Kingdom	44
Japan	81	Uruguay	598
Jordan	962	Venezuela	58
Kenya, Rep of	254	Zaire, Rep of	243
Korea Rep of [South]	82	Zimbabwe	263

Dial 011 + Country Code + City Code + Local Number

Calls to Canada, Puerto Rico, and many Caribbean countries are dialed the same way as long-distance calls within the United States. You only need to dial "1" + area code + number. No international access codes are required.

U.S. Area Codes

Alabama
Birmingham 205
Huntsville 256
Mobile 251
Montgomery 334

Alaska 907

Arizona
Flagstaff 928
Phoenix 480/602/623
Tucson 520

Arkansas
Fayetteville 479
Jonesboro 870
Little Rock 501

California
Anaheim 714
Bakersfield 661
Burbank 818
Fresno 559
Irvine 949
Livermore 925
Long Beach 562
Los Angeles 213/323
Modesto 209
Monterey 831
Oakland 510
Ontario 909
Palm Springs 760
Palo Alto 650
Pasadena 626
Sacramento 530/916
San Diego 619/858
San Francisco 415
San Jose 408
Santa Barbara 805
Santa Monica 310
Santa Rosa 707

Colorado
Colorado Springs 719
Denver 303/720
Fort Collins 970

Connecticut 203/860

Delaware 302

District of Columbia 202

Florida
Boca Raton 561
Daytona Beach 386
Fort Lauderdale 754/954
Fort Myers 239
Fort Pierce 772
Gainesville 352
Jacksonville 904
Lakeland 863
Miami 786/305
Orlando 321/407
Sarasota 941
St. Petersburg 727
Tallahassee 850
Tampa 813

Georgia
Albany 229

Atlanta 404/470/678
Columbus 706/762
Macon 478
Marietta 770
Savannah 912

Hawaii 808

Idaho 208

Illinois
Aurora 630/331
Chicago 312/773
Cicero 708
Collinsville 618
Peoria 309
Rockford 815/779
Springfield 217
Waukegan 847/224

Indiana
Evansville 812
Fort Wayne 260
Gary .219
Indianapolis 317
Lafayette 765
South Bend 574

Iowa
Cedar Rapids 319
Des Moines 515
Dubuque 563
Marshalltown 641
Sioux City 712

Kansas
Dodge City 620
Kansas City 913
Topeka 785
Wichita 316

Kentucky
Ashland 606
Lexington 859
Louisville 270/502

Louisiana
Baton Rouge 225
Lafayette 337
New Orleans 504/985
Shreveport 318

Maine 207

Maryland
Baltimore 410/443
Silver Springs 301/240

Massachusetts
Boston 617/857/781/339
Cape Cod/Worcester 508/774
Lowell 351/978
Springfield 413

Michigan
Ann Arbor 734
Detroit 313
Flint .810
Grand Rapids 616
Kalamazoo 269
Lansing 517

Muskegon 231
Pontiac 248/947
Saginaw 989
Sault Ste. Marie 906
Warren 586

Minnesota
Duluth 218
Minneapolis 612/763/952
Rochester 507
St. Cloud 320
St. Paul 651

Mississippi
Biloxi 228
Jackson 601/769
Tupelo 662

Missouri
Jefferson City 573
Kansas City 816
Sedalia 660
Springfield 417
St. Charles 636
St. Louis 314

Montana 406

Nebraska
North Platte 308
Omaha 402

Nevada
Las Vegas 702
Reno 775

New Hampshire 603

New Jersey
Camden 856
Elizabeth 908
Hackensack 201/551
New Brunswick 732/848
Newark 862/973
Trenton 609

New Mexico 505/575

New York
Albany 518
Binghamton 607
Buffalo 716
Long Island 516
New York City 917
NYC: Bronx, Brooklyn,
Queens & Staten Island . .347/718
NYC: Manhattan 212/646
Poughkeepsie 845
Rochester 585
Syracuse 315
White Plains 914

North Carolina
Asheville 828
Cape Hatteras 252
Charlotte 704/980
Fayetteville 910
Raleigh 919
Winston-Salem 336

North Dakota 701

For long-distance information, dial 1+ (Area Code) 555-1212. When requiring an unknown Area Code for a particular place, dial "0" (Local Operator).

Time Zones and Phone Area Codes

AREA CODES & TIME ZONES

© 2006 *MAPS*.com

* Arizona and Hawaii do not participate in Daylight Saving Time. Therefore, during Daylight Saving Time (March to November), these states' time zones will be one hour earlier than shown.

Ohio
Cincinnati 513
Cleveland 216
Columbus 614
Dayton 937
Lorain 440
Toledo 419/567
Youngstown 330/234
Zanesville 740

Oklahoma
Lawton 580
Oklahoma City 405
Tulsa 918

Oregon
Eugene 541
Portland/Salem 503/971

Pennsylvania
Allentown 610/484
Erie 814
Harrisburg 717
New Castle 724/878
Philadelphia 267/215
Pittsburgh 412/878
Scranton 570

Rhode Island 401

South Carolina
Charleston 843

Columbia 803
Greenville 864

South Dakota 605

Tennessee
Chattanooga 423
Clarksville 931
Jackson 731
Knoxville 865
Memphis 901
Nashville 615

Texas
Abilene 325
Amarillo 806
Austin 512
Corpus Christi 361
Dallas 469/972/214
Del Rio 830
Denton 940
El Paso 915
Fort Worth 682/817
Galveston 409
Houston 832/281/713
Huntsville 936
Laredo 956
Midland/Odessa 432
San Antonio 210
Tyler 903/430
Waco 254

Utah 435
Salt Lake City 801

Vermont 802

Virginia
Arlington 703/571
Bristol 276
Harrisonburg 540
Lynchburg 434
Richmond 804
Virginia Beach 757

Washington
Bellevue 425
Bellingham/Olympia 360
Seattle 206/564
Spokane 509
Tacoma 253

West Virginia 304

Wisconsin
Eau Claire 715
Green Bay 920
Madison 608
Milwaukee 414
Racine 262

Wyoming 307

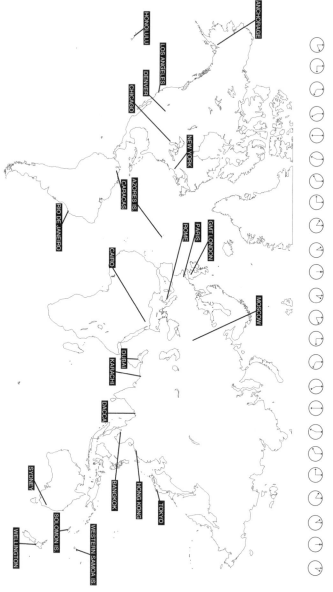

World Map and Time Zones

256

Web Sites

Car Rentals

Alamo . . . . .www.alamo.com
Avis . . . . .www.avis.com
Budget . . . . .www.budget.com
Dollar . . . . .www.dollar.com
Hertz . . . . .www.hertz.com
National . . . .www.nationalcar.com
Thrifty . . . . .www.thrifty.com

Airlines

Air Canada . . . .www.aircanada.com
American . . . . .www.aa.com
America West . . .www.usairways.com
British Airways . . . .
. . . . .www.britishairways.com
Continental . .www.continental.com
Delta . . . . .www.delta.com
Japan Airlines . . . .www.jal.co.jp/en/
Northwest/KLM . . . .www.nwa.com
Southwest Airlines . . . .
. . . . .www.southwest.com
US Air . . . . . . .www.usairways.com
United . . . . .www.united.com

Credit Cards

American Express . . . .
. . . . . . .www.americanexpress.com
Discover Card . . . .
. . . . .www.discovercard.com
Master Card . .www.mastercard.com
Visa . . . . .www.visa.com

Delivery/Shipping

DHL . . . . .www.dhl.com
FedEx . . . . .www.fedex.com
UPS . . . . .www.ups.com

Hotels

Best Western . .www.bestwestern.com
Comfort Inn . .www.choicehotels.com
Doubletree . . .www.doubletree.com
Econo Lodges . . . .
. . . . .www.choicehotels.com
Embassy Suites . . . .
. . . . .www.embassysuites.com
Fairmont . . . . . .www.fairmont.com
Hampton Inn www.hamptoninn.com
Hilton . . . . .www.hilton.com
Holiday Inns . . www.holidayinn.com
Hyatt Hotels . . . . . .www.hyatt.com
InterContinental . . . .
. . . . .www.ichotelsgroup.com
Marriott Hotels . .www.marriott.com
Omni Hotels .www.omnihotels.com
Radisson . . . . . . .www.radisson.com
Ramada Inns . . . .www.ramada.com
Sheraton Hotels . . . .
. . . . .www.starwoodhotels.com
Sonesta Hotels . .www.sonesta.com
Studio Plus . . . .www.studioplus.com
Travelodge . . . .www.travelodge.com
Westin . . . . .www.westin.com

Frequently Used Web Sites

Company	Web Site
Company	Web Site
Company	Web Site
Company	Web Site
Company	Web Site
Company	Web Site
Company	Web Site
Company	Web Site
Company	Web Site
Company	Web Site
Company	Web Site
Company	Web Site
Company	Web Site
Company	Web Site
Company	Web Site
Company	Web Site
Company	Web Site
Company	Web Site
Company	Web Site
Company	Web Site
Company	Web Site
Company	Web Site
Company	Web Site
Company	Web Site
Company	Web Site
Company	Web Site
Company	Web Site
Company	Web Site

A

Name		Name
Address		Address

| Telephone | | Telephone |
| E-mail | | E-mail |

| Name | | Name |
| Address | | Address |

| Telephone | | Telephone |
| E-mail | | E-mail |

| Name | | Name |
| Address | | Address |

| Telephone | | Telephone |
| E-mail | | E-mail |

| Name | | Name |
| Address | | Address |

| Telephone | | Telephone |
| E-mail | | E-mail |

| Name | | Name |
| Address | | Address |

| Telephone | | Telephone |
| E-mail | | E-mail |

B

Name

Address

Telephone

E-mail

Name

Address

Telephone

E-mail

Name

Address

Telephone

E-mail

Name

Address

Telephone

E-mail

Name

Address

Telephone

E-mail

Name

Address

Telephone

E-mail

Name

Address

Telephone

E-mail

Name

Address

Telephone

E-mail

Name

Address

Telephone

E-mail

Name

Address

Telephone

E-mail

C

Name	*Name*
Address	*Address*
Telephone	*Telephone*
E-mail	*E-mail*
Name	*Name*
Address	*Address*
Telephone	*Telephone*
E-mail	*E-mail*
Name	*Name*
Address	*Address*
Telephone	*Telephone*
E-mail	*E-mail*
Name	*Name*
Address	*Address*
Telephone	*Telephone*
E-mail	*E-mail*
Name	*Name*
Address	*Address*
Telephone	*Telephone*
E-mail	*E-mail*

D

Name	*Name*
Address	*Address*
Telephone	*Telephone*
E-mail	*E-mail*
Name	*Name*
Address	*Address*
Telephone	*Telephone*
E-mail	*E-mail*
Name	*Name*
Address	*Address*
Telephone	*Telephone*
E-mail	*E-mail*
Name	*Name*
Address	*Address*
Telephone	*Telephone*
E-mail	*E-mail*
Name	*Name*
Address	*Address*
Telephone	*Telephone*
E-mail	*E-mail*

EF

Name	Name
Address	Address
Telephone	Telephone
E-mail	E-mail

Name	Name
Address	Address
Telephone	Telephone
E-mail	E-mail

Name	Name
Address	Address
Telephone	Telephone
E-mail	E-mail

Name	Name
Address	Address
Telephone	Telephone
E-mail	E-mail

Name	Name
Address	Address
Telephone	Telephone
E-mail	E-mail

G

Name	*Name*
Address	*Address*
Telephone	*Telephone*
E-mail	*E-mail*
Name	*Name*
Address	*Address*
Telephone	*Telephone*
E-mail	*E-mail*
Name	*Name*
Address	*Address*
Telephone	*Telephone*
E-mail	*E-mail*
Name	*Name*
Address	*Address*
Telephone	*Telephone*
E-mail	*E-mail*
Name	*Name*
Address	*Address*
Telephone	*Telephone*
E-mail	*E-mail*

Name

Address

Telephone

E-mail

Name

Address

Telephone

E-mail

Name

Address

Telephone

E-mail

Name

Address

Telephone

E-mail

Name

Address

Telephone

E-mail

Name

Address

Telephone

E-mail

Name

Address

Telephone

E-mail

Name

Address

Telephone

E-mail

Name

Address

Telephone

E-mail

Name

Address

Telephone

E-mail

I J

Name	*Name*
Address	*Address*
Telephone	*Telephone*
E-mail	*E-mail*
Name	*Name*
Address	*Address*
Telephone	*Telephone*
E-mail	*E-mail*
Name	*Name*
Address	*Address*
Telephone	*Telephone*
E-mail	*E-mail*
Name	*Name*
Address	*Address*
Telephone	*Telephone*
E-mail	*E-mail*
Name	*Name*
Address	*Address*
Telephone	*Telephone*
E-mail	*E-mail*

K

Name

Address

Telephone

E-mail

Name

Address

Telephone

E-mail

Name

Address

Telephone

E-mail

Name

Address

Telephone

E-mail

Name

Address

Telephone

E-mail

Name

Address

Telephone

E-mail

Name

Address

Telephone

E-mail

Name

Address

Telephone

E-mail

Name

Address

Telephone

E-mail

Name

Address

Telephone

E-mail

L

Name	*Name*
Address	*Address*
Telephone	*Telephone*
E-mail	*E-mail*
Name	*Name*
Address	*Address*
Telephone	*Telephone*
E-mail	*E-mail*
Name	*Name*
Address	*Address*
Telephone	*Telephone*
E-mail	*E-mail*
Name	*Name*
Address	*Address*
Telephone	*Telephone*
E-mail	*E-mail*
Name	*Name*
Address	*Address*
Telephone	*Telephone*
E-mail	*E-mail*

M

Name	*Name*
Address	*Address*
Telephone	*Telephone*
E-mail	*E-mail*
Name	*Name*
Address	*Address*
Telephone	*Telephone*
E-mail	*E-mail*
Name	*Name*
Address	*Address*
Telephone	*Telephone*
E-mail	*E-mail*
Name	*Name*
Address	*Address*
Telephone	*Telephone*
E-mail	*E-mail*
Name	*Name*
Address	*Address*
Telephone	*Telephone*
E-mail	*E-mail*

N

Name

Address

Telephone

E-mail

Name

Address

Telephone

E-mail

Name

Address

Telephone

E-mail

Name

Address

Telephone

E-mail

Name

Address

Telephone

E-mail

Name

Address

Telephone

E-mail

Name

Address

Telephone

E-mail

Name

Address

Telephone

E-mail

Name

Address

Telephone

E-mail

Name

Address

Telephone

E-mail

Name

Address

Telephone

E-mail

Name

Address

Telephone

E-mail

Name

Address

Telephone

E-mail

Name

Address

Telephone

E-mail

Name

Address

Telephone

E-mail

Name

Address

Telephone

E-mail

Name

Address

Telephone

E-mail

Name

Address

Telephone

E-mail

Name

Address

Telephone

E-mail

Name

Address

Telephone

E-mail

P

Name

Address

Telephone

E-mail

Name

Address

Telephone

E-mail

Name

Address

Telephone

E-mail

Name

Address

Telephone

E-mail

Name

Address

Telephone

E-mail

Name

Address

Telephone

E-mail

Name

Address

Telephone

E-mail

Name

Address

Telephone

E-mail

Name

Address

Telephone

E-mail

Name

Address

Telephone

E-mail

Name

Name

Address

Address

Telephone

Telephone

E-mail

E-mail

Name

Name

Address

Address

Telephone

Telephone

E-mail

E-mail

Name

Name

Address

Address

Telephone

Telephone

E-mail

E-mail

Name

Name

Address

Address

Telephone

Telephone

E-mail

E-mail

Name

Name

Address

Address

Telephone

Telephone

E-mail

E-mail

S

Name	*Name*
Address	*Address*
Telephone	*Telephone*
E-mail	*E-mail*
Name	*Name*
Address	*Address*
Telephone	*Telephone*
E-mail	*E-mail*
Name	*Name*
Address	*Address*
Telephone	*Telephone*
E-mail	*E-mail*
Name	*Name*
Address	*Address*
Telephone	*Telephone*
E-mail	*E-mail*
Name	*Name*
Address	*Address*
Telephone	*Telephone*
E-mail	*E-mail*

T

Name

Address

Telephone

E-mail

Name

Address

Telephone

E-mail

Name

Address

Telephone

E-mail

Name

Address

Telephone

E-mail

Name

Address

Telephone

E-mail

Name

Address

Telephone

E-mail

Name

Address

Telephone

E-mail

Name

Address

Telephone

E-mail

Name

Address

Telephone

E-mail

Name

Address

Telephone

E-mail

UV

Name

Address

Telephone

E-mail

Name

Address

Telephone

E-mail

Name

Address

Telephone

E-mail

Name

Address

Telephone

E-mail

Name

Address

Telephone

E-mail

Name

Address

Telephone

E-mail

Name

Address

Telephone

E-mail

Name

Address

Telephone

E-mail

Name

Address

Telephone

E-mail

Name

Address

Telephone

E-mail

Name	Name
Address	Address
Telephone	Telephone
E-mail	E-mail
Name	Name
Address	Address
Telephone	Telephone
E-mail	E-mail
Name	Name
Address	Address
Telephone	Telephone
E-mail	E-mail
Name	Name
Address	Address
Telephone	Telephone
E-mail	E-mail
Name	Name
Address	Address
Telephone	Telephone
E-mail	E-mail

XYZ

Name	*Name*
Address	*Address*
Telephone	*Telephone*
E-mail	*E-mail*
Name	*Name*
Address	*Address*
Telephone	*Telephone*
E-mail	*E-mail*
Name	*Name*
Address	*Address*
Telephone	*Telephone*
E-mail	*E-mail*
Name	*Name*
Address	*Address*
Telephone	*Telephone*
E-mail	*E-mail*
Name	*Name*
Address	*Address*
Telephone	*Telephone*
E-mail	*E-mail*

Crisis Scripture Guide

ADDICTION	Galatians 5:1; John 8:32; Proverbs 20:1
AGING	Proverbs 9:11; Ecclesiastes 11:10; Proverbs 10:27
ANGER	1 Peter 2:23; Ephesians 4:26–27; 1 Thessalonians 5:9
ANXIETY	John 14:27; Philippians 4:6–8; Psalm 46:1–3
BACKSLIDING	Proverbs 28:13; Psalm 51:10–12; John 6:37
BEREAVEMENT	1 Corinthians 15:54–57; Isaiah 25:8; 1 Thessalonians 4:13–14
BITTERNESS	Ephesians 4:31; Hebrews 12:15; James 3:14–15
CARNALITY	Romans 6:6–9; Ephesians 4:22–24; 2 Corinthians 4:16
CONDEMNATION	Romans 8:1; Romans 3:10–12; Isaiah 64:6–8
CONFUSION	Isaiah 26:3; 1 Corinthians 14:33; Isaiah 55:8–9
DEATH	Romans 14:7–8; Job 19:25–27; Isaiah 25:8
DEPRESSION	Nehemiah 8:10; Philippians 4:8; Romans 8:28
DISSATISFACTION	Proverbs 27:20; Hebrews 13:5–6; 1 Timothy 6:6–8
DOUBT	James 4:8; Romans 10:17; Hebrews 10:32, 35–39
FAILURE	Proverbs 24:16–18; Psalm 145:14–16; 2 Corinthians 3:5
FEAR	2 Timothy 1:7; Philippians 4:13; Revelation 1:17–18
FINANCES	Matthew 6:31–34; Psalm 37:25–26; Philippians 4:19
ILLNESS	James 5:14; Psalm 23:2–4; Psalm 43:5
INSECURITY	2 Thessalonians 3:3; Psalm 91:3–7; 2 Corinthians 3:4–5
JUDGING	1 Corinthians 4:5; Matthew 7:3–5; John 5:22
LONELINESS	John 14:18; Psalm 147:3; Psalm 27:10
LUST	2 Peter 2:9; Matthew 18:8–9; Proverbs 6:25–26
MARRIAGE	2 Corinthians 6:14–17; 1 Corinthians 7:10–17; Hebrews 13:4
PRIDE	Matthew 18:2–4; Proverbs 27:1–2; Luke 18:11–14
SATAN	Ephesians 6:10–17; 1 John 4:1–3; Luke 10:18–19
SUFFERING	Hebrews 5:8–9; 2 Corinthians 4:8–10; 1 Peter 4:19
TEMPTATION	James 1:12; 2 Peter 2:9; James 1:2–4
TRIALS	2 Timothy 2:3; 1 Peter 4:12–13; Psalm 34:17
WEAKNESS	2 Corinthians 12:9; Matthew 11:28–30; Psalm 121:2–3
WORLDLINESS	Mark 4:18–20; 1 John 5:5; 1 John 2:15–17

Prayers of Praise

Enter into His gates with thanksgiving, And into His courts with praise. Be thankful to Him, and bless His name. Psalm 100:4

_____

_____

_____

_____

_____

_____

_____

_____

_____

Prayers of Confession

If we confess our sins, He is faithful and just to forgive us our sins and to cleanse us from all unrighteousness. 1 John 1:9

_____

_____

_____

_____

_____

_____

_____

_____

_____

Prayers of Forgiveness

For if you forgive men their trespasses, your heavenly Father will also forgive you. Matthew 6:14

_____

_____

_____

_____

_____

_____

_____

_____

_____

_____

Prayers of Petition

Be anxious for nothing, but in everything by prayer and supplication, with thanksgiving, let your requests be made known to God. Philippians 4:6

_____

_____

_____

_____

_____

_____

_____

_____

_____

Prayers of Intercession

Confess your tresspasses to one another, and pray for one another, that you may be healed. The effective, fervent prayer of a righteous man avails much. James 5:16

Prayers of Faith

But without faith it is impossible to please Him, for he who comes to God must believe that He is, and that He is a rewarder of those who diligently seek Him. Hebrews 11:6

Prayers of Consistency

Evening and morning and at noon I will pray, and cry aloud,
And He shall hear my voice. Psalm 55:17

_____

_____

_____

_____

_____

_____

_____

_____

_____

_____

Prayers of Agreement

Again I say to you that if two of you agree on earth concerning
anything that they ask, it will be done for them by My Father in
heaven. Matthew 18:19

_____

_____

_____

_____

_____

_____

_____

_____

_____

_____

Prayer Journal

One-Year Bible Reading Schedule

✓	Day	Scripture	✓	Day	Scripture	✓	Day	Scripture
❏	1	Genesis 1–3	❏	44	Leviticus 1–3	❏	86	Deut. 19–21
❏	2	Genesis 4–6	❏	45	Leviticus 4–6	❏	87	Deut. 22–24
❏	3	Genesis 7–9	❏	46	Leviticus 7–9	❏	88	Deut. 25–27
❏	4	Genesis 10–12	❏	47	Leviticus 10–12	❏	89	Deut. 28–30
❏	5	Genesis 13–15	❏	48	Leviticus 13–15	❏	90	Deut. 31–34
❏	6	Genesis 16–18	❏	49	Leviticus 16–18			
❏	7	Genesis 19–21	❏	50	Leviticus 19–21	❏	91	Acts 1–3
❏	8	Genesis 22–24	❏	51	Leviticus 22–24	❏	92	Acts 4–6
❏	9	Genesis 25–27	❏	52	Leviticus 25–27	❏	93	Acts 7–9
❏	10	Genesis 28–30				❏	94	Acts 10–12
❏	11	Genesis 31–33	❏	53	Luke 1–3	❏	95	Acts 13–15
❏	12	Genesis 34–36	❏	54	Luke 4–6	❏	96	Acts 16–18
❏	13	Genesis 37–39	❏	55	Luke 7–9	❏	97	Acts 19–21
❏	14	Genesis 40–42	❏	56	Luke 10–12	❏	98	Acts 22–24
❏	15	Genesis 43–45	❏	57	Luke 13–15	❏	99	Acts 25–28
❏	16	Genesis 46–50	❏	58	Luke 16–18			
			❏	59	Luke 19–21	❏	100	Joshua 1–3
❏	17	Matthew 1–3	❏	60	Luke 22–24	❏	101	Joshua 4–6
❏	18	Matthew 4–6				❏	102	Joshua 7–9
❏	19	Matthew 7–9	❏	61	Numbers 1–3	❏	103	Joshua 10–12
❏	20	Matthew 10–12	❏	62	Numbers 4–6	❏	104	Joshua 13–15
❏	21	Matthew 13–15	❏	63	Numbers 7–9	❏	105	Joshua 16–18
❏	22	Matthew 16–18	❏	64	Numbers 10–12	❏	106	Joshua 19–21
❏	23	Matthew 19–21	❏	65	Numbers 13–15	❏	107	Joshua 22–24
❏	24	Matthew 22–24	❏	66	Numbers 16–18			
❏	25	Matthew 25–28	❏	67	Numbers 19–21	❏	108	Romans 1–3
			❏	68	Numbers 22–24	❏	109	Romans 4–6
❏	26	Exodus 1–3	❏	69	Numbers 25–27	❏	110	Romans 7–9
❏	27	Exodus 4–6	❏	70	Numbers 28–30	❏	111	Romans 10–12
❏	28	Exodus 7–9	❏	71	Numbers 31–33	❏	112	Romans 13–16
❏	29	Exodus 10–12	❏	72	Numbers 34–36			
❏	30	Exodus 13–15				❏	113	Judges 1–3
❏	31	Exodus 16–18	❏	73	John 1–3	❏	114	Judges 4–6
❏	32	Exodus 19–21	❏	74	John 4–6	❏	115	Judges 7–9
❏	33	Exodus 22–24	❏	75	John 7–9	❏	116	Judges 10–12
❏	34	Exodus 25–27	❏	76	John 10–12	❏	117	Judges 13–15
❏	35	Exodus 28–30	❏	77	John 13–15	❏	118	Judges 16–18
❏	36	Exodus 31–33	❏	78	John 16–18	❏	119	Judges 19–21
❏	37	Exodus 34–36	❏	79	John 19–21			
❏	38	Exodus 37–40				❏	120	Ruth 1–2
			❏	80	Deut. 1–3	❏	121	Ruth 3–4
❏	39	Mark 1–3	❏	81	Deut. 4–6			
❏	40	Mark 4–6	❏	82	Deut. 7–9	❏	122	1 Corinthians 1–3
❏	41	Mark 7–9	❏	83	Deut. 10–12	❏	123	1 Corinthians 4–6
❏	42	Mark 10–12	❏	84	Deut. 13–15	❏	124	1 Corinthians 7–9
❏	43	Mark 13–16	❏	85	Deut. 16–18	❏	125	1 Corinthians 10–12
						❏	126	1 Corinthians 13–16

One-Year Bible Reading Schedule

✓	Day	Scripture
❏	127	1 Samuel 1–3
❏	128	1 Samuel 4–6
❏	129	1 Samuel 7–9
❏	130	1 Samuel 10–12
❏	131	1 Samuel 13–15
❏	132	1 Samuel 16–18
❏	133	1 Samuel 19–21
❏	134	1 Samuel 22–24
❏	135	1 Samuel 25–27
❏	136	1 Samuel 28–31
❏	137	2 Corinthians 1–3
❏	138	2 Corinthians 4–6
❏	139	2 Corinthians 7–9
❏	140	2 Corinthians 10–13
❏	141	2 Samuel 1–3
❏	142	2 Samuel 4–6
❏	143	2 Samuel 7–9
❏	144	2 Samuel 10–12
❏	145	2 Samuel 13–15
❏	146	2 Samuel 16–18
❏	147	2 Samuel 19–21
❏	148	2 Samuel 22–24
❏	149	Galatians 1–3
❏	150	Galatians 4–6
❏	151	1 Kings 1–3
❏	152	1 Kings 4–6
❏	153	1 Kings 7–9
❏	154	1 Kings 10–12
❏	155	1 Kings 13–15
❏	156	1 Kings 16–18
❏	157	1 Kings 19–22
❏	158	Ephesians 1–3
❏	159	Ephesians 4–6
❏	160	2 Kings 1–3
❏	161	2 Kings 4–6
❏	162	2 Kings 7–9
❏	163	2 Kings 10–12
❏	164	2 Kings 13–15
❏	165	2 Kings 16–18
❏	166	2 Kings 19–21
❏	167	2 Kings 22–25

✓	Day	Scripture
❏	168	Philippians 1–4
❏	169	1 Chronicles 1–3
❏	170	1 Chronicles 4–6
❏	171	1 Chronicles 7–9
❏	172	1 Chronicles 10–12
❏	173	1 Chronicles 13–15
❏	174	1 Chronicles 16–18
❏	175	1 Chronicles 19–21
❏	176	1 Chronicles 22–24
❏	177	1 Chronicles 25–27
❏	178	1 Chronicles 28–29
❏	179	Colossians 1–4
❏	180	2 Chronicles 1–3
❏	181	2 Chronicles 4–6
❏	182	2 Chronicles 7–9
❏	183	2 Chronicles 10–12
❏	184	2 Chronicles 13–15
❏	185	2 Chronicles 16–18
❏	186	2 Chronicles 19–21
❏	187	2 Chronicles 22–24
❏	188	2 Chronicles 25–27
❏	189	2 Chronicles 28–30
❏	190	2 Chronicles 31–33
❏	191	2 Chronicles 34–36
❏	192	1 Thessalonians 1–5
❏	193	2 Thessalonians 1–3
❏	194	Ezra 1–3
❏	195	Ezra 4–6
❏	196	Ezra 7–10
❏	197	Nehemiah 1–3
❏	198	Nehemiah 4–6
❏	199	Nehemiah 7–9
❏	200	Nehemiah 10–13
❏	201	Esther 1–3
❏	202	Esther 4–6
❏	203	Esther 7–10
❏	204	Job 1–4
❏	205	Job 5–8
❏	206	Job 9–12

✓	Day	Scripture
❏	207	Job 13–16
❏	208	Job 17–21
❏	209	Job 22–26
❏	210	Job 27–30
❏	211	Job 31–34
❏	212	Job 35–38
❏	213	Job 39–42
❏	214	1 Timothy 1–3
❏	215	1 Timothy 4–6
❏	216	2 Timothy 1–4
❏	217	Psalms 1–5
❏	218	Psalms 6–10
❏	219	Psalms 11–15
❏	220	Psalms 16–20
❏	221	Psalms 21–25
❏	222	Psalms 26–30
❏	223	Psalms 31–34
❏	224	Psalms 35–37
❏	225	Psalms 38–41
❏	226	Psalms 42–45
❏	227	Psalms 46–49
❏	228	Psalms 50–53
❏	229	Psalms 54–57
❏	230	Psalms 58–61
❏	231	Psalms 62–65
❏	232	Psalms 66–68
❏	233	Psalms 69–72
❏	234	Psalms 73–76
❏	235	Psalms 77–78
❏	236	Psalms 79–82
❏	237	Psalms 83–86
❏	238	Psalms 87–89
❏	239	Psalms 90–93
❏	240	Psalms 94–97
❏	241	Psalms 98–102
❏	242	Psalms 103–104
❏	243	Psalms 105–106
❏	244	Psalms 107–109
❏	245	Psalms 110–115
❏	246	Psalms 116–118
❏	247	Psalms 119:1–88
❏	248	Psalms 119:89–176

One-Year Bible Reading Schedule

✓ Day	Scripture
❑ 249	Psalms 120–127
❑ 250	Psalms 128–134
❑ 251	Psalms 135–138
❑ 252	Psalms 139–142
❑ 253	Psalms 143–146
❑ 254	Psalms 147–150
❑ 255	Titus, Philemon
❑ 256	Proverbs 1–4
❑ 257	Proverbs 5–8
❑ 258	Proverbs 9–12
❑ 259	Proverbs 13–15
❑ 260	Proverbs 16–18
❑ 261	Proverbs 19–21
❑ 262	Proverbs 22–24
❑ 263	Proverbs 25–27
❑ 264	Proverbs 28–31
❑ 265	Hebrews 1–4
❑ 266	Hebrews 5–7
❑ 267	Hebrews 8–10
❑ 268	Hebrews 11–13
❑ 269	Ecclesiastes 1–4
❑ 270	Eccesiastes 5–8
❑ 271	Ecclesiastes 9–12
❑ 272	S. of S. 1–2
❑ 273	S. of S. 3–4
❑ 274	S. of S. 5–8
❑ 275	James 1–5
❑ 276	Isaiah 1–3
❑ 277	Isaiah 4–7
❑ 278	Isaiah 8–10
❑ 279	Isaiah 11–13
❑ 280	Isaiah 14–17
❑ 281	Isaiah 18–21
❑ 282	Isaiah 22–25
❑ 283	Isaiah 26–28
❑ 284	Isaiah 29–30
❑ 285	Isaiah 31–33
❑ 286	Isaiah 34–36
❑ 287	Isaiah 37–39
❑ 288	Isaiah 40–42

✓ Day	Scripture
❑ 289	Isaiah 43–45
❑ 290	Isaiah 46–48
❑ 291	Isaiah 49–51
❑ 292	Isaiah 52–54
❑ 293	Isaiah 55–57
❑ 294	Isaiah 58–60
❑ 295	Isaiah 61–63
❑ 296	Isaiah 64–66
❑ 297	1 Peter 1–5
❑ 298	Jeremiah 1–3
❑ 299	Jeremiah 4–6
❑ 300	Jeremiah 7–9
❑ 301	Jeremiah 10–12
❑ 302	Jeremiah 13–15
❑ 303	Jeremiah 16–18
❑ 304	Jeremiah 19–21
❑ 305	Jeremiah 22–24
❑ 306	Jeremiah 25–27
❑ 307	Jeremiah 28–30
❑ 308	Jeremiah 31–33
❑ 309	Jeremiah 34–36
❑ 310	Jeremiah 37–39
❑ 311	Jeremiah 40–42
❑ 312	Jeremiah 43–45
❑ 313	Jeremiah 46–48
❑ 314	Jeremiah 49–52
❑ 315	2 Peter 1–3
❑ 316	Lamentations 1–3
❑ 317	Lamentations 4–5
❑ 318	Ezekiel 1–4
❑ 319	Ezekiel 5–8
❑ 320	Ezekiel 9–12
❑ 321	Ezekiel 13–15
❑ 322	Ezekiel 16–18
❑ 323	Ezekiel 19–21
❑ 324	Ezekiel 22–24
❑ 325	Ezekiel 25–27
❑ 326	Ezekiel 28–30
❑ 327	Ezekiel 31–33
❑ 328	Ezekiel 34–36
❑ 329	Ezekiel 37–39

✓ Day	Scripture
❑ 330	Ezekiel 40–42
❑ 331	Ezekiel 43–45
❑ 332	Ezekiel 46–48
❑ 333	1 John 1–5
❑ 334	Daniel 1–3
❑ 335	Daniel 4–6
❑ 336	Daniel 7–9
❑ 337	Daniel 10–12
❑ 338	Hosea 1–3
❑ 339	Hosea 4–6
❑ 340	Hosea 7–9
❑ 341	Hosea 10–12
❑ 342	Hosea 13–14
❑ 343	Joel 1–3
❑ 344	Amos 1–3
❑ 345	Amos 4–6
❑ 346	Amos 7–9
❑ 347	Obadiah
❑ 348	2 & 3 John, Jude
❑ 349	Jonah 1–4
❑ 350	Micah 1–3
❑ 351	Micah 4–7
❑ 352	Nahum 1–3
❑ 353	Habukkuk 1–3
❑ 354	Zephaniah, Hag.
❑ 355	Zechariah 1–3
❑ 356	Zechariah 4–6
❑ 357	Zechariah 7–9
❑ 358	Zechariah 10–14
❑ 359	Malachi 1–4
❑ 360	Revelation 1–3
❑ 361	Revelation 4–6
❑ 362	Revelation 7–10
❑ 363	Revelation 11–15
❑ 364	Revelation 16–18
❑ 365	Revelation 19–22